Advance Praise for *SLAY the Bully*

"The magic of Rebecca's SLAY approach to negotiating with narcisissts is her depth of understanding of the psychological mind of a narcissist. She seamlessly and efficiently integrates that understanding with her unique insight and skill level in the negotiating process. What Rebecca is offering you here is an opportunity and a path to create a solution for you, and ultimately for your life that will allow you to achieve something incredibly valuable: peace of mind. This is an opportunity. Embrace it."

—Chris Voss, co-author of
Never Split the Difference

"SLAY the Bully is a complete game changer! This book not only plunges into the minds of how narcissists think, reaching deep into their psyches, and pulling back the curtain on their personas, but also provides a real roadmap, complete with easy to follow strategies and tactics, to achieve the winning result you want when negotiating with a narcissist."

—Jon Gordon, *Wall Street Journal*
bestselling author of
The Energy Bus and *The Power of Positive Leadership*

"Narcissists big and small cause countless problems and toxicity that never ends. Here at last is a wisely brilliant lady and my friend, Rebecca Zung, who shares with us how to successfully confront and navigate through this seemingly intractable problem."

—Mark Victor Hansen, *New York Times* bestselling author, founder, and co-creator of the *Chicken Soup for the Soul* series

"When it comes to negotiation, confidence is critical. Rebecca has a powerful methodology that not only provides readers with the practical skills needed for success, but equips them with the tools for building the confidence to apply those skills when the stakes are high. By rooting her approach in foundational psychological concepts, she is helping millions of people advocate for themselves against the most difficult of personalities and enhance their sense of self-worth, all while negotiating for the things they want most. This book is a must-read for anyone ready to achieve new levels of success and empowerment."

—Kwame Christian, Esq. Founder, American Negotiation Institute, Author of *Finding Confidence in Conflict*, and Host of Negotiate Anything Podcast

SLAY®

HOW TO NEGOTIATE THE BULLY WITH A NARCISSIST AND WIN

REBECCA ZUNG, ESQ.

Foreword by Chris Voss

A SAVIO REPUBLIC BOOK
An Imprint of Post Hill Press
ISBN: 978-1-63758-686-0
ISBN (eBook): 978-1-63758-687-7

SLAY® the Bully:
How to Negotiate with a Narcissist and Win

Cover Design by Tiffani Shea

Although every effort has been made to ensure that the personal and professional advice present within this book is useful and appropriate, the author and publisher do not assume and hereby disclaim any liability to any person, business, or organization choosing to employ the guidance offered in this book.

The information provided herein shall not be construed as legal or psychological advice. For advice specific to your situation, please consult a licensed attorney or psychologist in your specific jurisdiction.

All people, locations, events, and situations are portrayed to the best of the author's memory. While all of the events described are true, many names and identifying details have been changed to protect the privacy of the people involved.

posthillpress.com
New York • Nashville
Published in the United States of America

4 5 6 7 8 9 10

TABLE OF CONTENTS

For all survivors of narcissists and bullies around the world

FOREWORD

By Chris Voss

I was nervous, of course.

But I couldn't show it. You can't show bad guys fear.

It was my very first negotiation with real hostages during a bank robbery. This was many years ago now, but I still remember it like it was yesterday. I got the call, and within a few minutes, I found myself at the corner of Seventh Avenue and Carroll Street in Brooklyn, New York, outside the Chase Manhattan Bank.

Still pretty green, I was out of negotiation training for barely a year. But there I was, facing the bad guys, one wingman and one "Lead Bad Guy." Lead Bad Guy—a highly shrewd, manipulative personality—decided that that day was going to be *his* day. His day to take control, his day to show who had the power.

Lead Bad Guy's decisions were deliberate, cold, and calculating. Lacking any and all integrity whatsoever, he didn't even bother sharing his day's plans with his own wingman. His wingman thought their afternoon was going to be a simple joyride of burglarizing the bank, probably followed by a spending spree somewhere.

By the time we got there, the two had taken two female bank tellers and a male security guard as hostages. One had been pistol whipped with a .357 Magnum revolver, and Lead Bad Guy had pretended to shoot another (although the gun wasn't loaded). Purely sadistic. Plain and simple.

Using brute-force negotiation tactics with hostage takers doesn't work. People can quickly end up dead that way. Hostage takers need to be influenced into surrendering, even though it may seem counterintuitive. Influencing hostage takers is a delicate process, one in which egos must be constantly navigated and where a continuous and healthy display of respect needs to be paid, or at least feels like it is being paid, to them.

On that day, after nearly twelve hours, we were able to convince both bad guys to surrender, and the hostages were safely released to us. Once the wingman gave himself up earlier in the day and shared details with us, their house of cards began to fall. A dramatic end to a very long day, to say the least.

There can be little doubt that hostage takers and narcissists have much in common. Often, they have delusional, grandiose fantasies of power. They are preoccupied with unreasonable expectations of admiration, they take advantage of others to get what they want, and of course, it goes without saying that they seemingly have no ability to recognize others' needs or feelings in the process.

You can't split the difference with hostage takers just like you can't split the difference with narcissists. Highly advanced negotiation skills are required when dealing with these people. That is precisely why I was drawn to Rebecca Zung and her SLAY method as set forth here in *SLAY the Bully: How to Negotiate with a Narcissist and Win.*

Rebecca and I share a common approach to dealing with highly complex, difficult personalities. The magic of her SLAY approach to negotiate with narcissists lies within her depth of understanding of the psychological mind of the narcissist (which can sometimes be sadistic, arbitrary, capricious, and even maniacal).

She seamlessly and efficiently integrates this understanding with her unique insight and skill in the negotiating process. She is then able to distill it all down and lay it out in a simple step-by-step structure that anyone can follow.

Narcissists and hostage takers are both types of people who want attention. They want their moment in the sun. For attention-seeking personality types, it is essential to create the illusion of control during the negotiation process in order to gain the upper hand on their egos. Trying to get your opponent to admit you're right is not only a futile process but also one that will simply enrage the other side and potentially cause communication to fail entirely. This is why Rebecca's framework is so incredibly useful.

The name of my company is The Black Swan Group. The Black Swan theory is this: things that were previously thought to be impossible can—and do—happen. In the negotiation context, it's being able to accomplish an outcome by uncovering information you didn't even know existed. These are the *unknown unknowns*, the difference that makes the difference in the end.

With SLAY, Rebecca has found a Black Swan. The majority of the population believes you can't negotiate with narcissists, but she has put together a framework that makes it not only possible, but probable to ensure a winning outcome. The bonus is that once you "SLAY" the narcissist, you can create a new mindset and thus, a new life. Whether a person's battle is personal or professional, the information in this book delivers insights every single one of us can use.

There are seemingly more narcissists in the world than ever right now. Ten years ago, I hardly ever heard this word, but now it seems to be an epidemic. This is not a problem that is going away anytime soon.

I have often said that every moment of life, every conversation, and every interaction with people is a negotiation—especially when you're dealing with a narcissist. The personal and professional costs can be great: emotionally, financially, physically, and spiritually. What Rebecca is offering you is an opportunity and a path to create a solution for you—and ultimately for your life—that will allow you to achieve something incredibly valuable: peace of mind.

This is an opportunity. Embrace it.

Chris Voss
Former FBI Lead Hostage Negotiator
CEO of The Black Swan Group
Wall Street Journal Bestselling Author of
Never Split the Difference

PREFACE

Bullies. Unfortunately, I know them well. And I know the *shame* of knowing them well.

For me, growing up in the 1970s was similar in many ways to many others' experiences of suburbia during that time.

I went to public school. I rode a big yellow school bus. I ate the school lunch. My brother and I were "latchkey" kids who watched reruns of *The Brady Bunch* and *Gilligan's Island* after school on the one color television we had in our house. The TV had four channels, which represented the major networks plus the one local public television station. We drank Kool-Aid with Red Dye No. 2, ran through sprinklers in our yard, and played Kick the Can on the street in front of our house.

But I was also very different. I was half-Chinese. I lived in Northern Virginia, just outside of Washington, DC, and racism was still quite prevalent there during that time. My parents were married in the 1960s, prior to the landmark U.S. Supreme Court case *Loving v. Virginia*, in which the Court ruled that the state laws banning interracial marriage were unconstitutional. This meant that because my mother was white and my father was Asian, it was actually *illegal* for them to marry in the Commonwealth of Virginia at the time when they wanted to get married, so my parents had their wedding ceremony in Washington, DC instead. I tell you all of this to give you an appreciation of the racial climate in the area at the time.

When my younger brother was born, just after me, my mother, who had been an operating room nurse, realized that my father, who had spent his life as an anesthesiologist, didn't have a lot of real estate knowledge, so she decided to get her real estate license to gain some understanding. Once she obtained it, she decided to go ahead and become a real estate salesperson. Her career immediately took off, and her life became much more about her business, as she then even started her own real estate company. My father would come home at the same time each day and make dinner and was, in a lot of ways, "our mother," but he was certainly not maternal. Thus, my brother and I were left on our own a lot of the time.

My father left quite early for the hospital each morning. This meant my brother and I had to get ourselves up, make our own breakfast (meaning, pour cereal out of a box and milk on top of it), and make our way to the bus stop.

Kids who don't have a whole lot of home support, whose moms aren't present, already feel very different from the kids who have moms at home all the time. Add in being the only kids who are half-Asian in an all-white community, and this really makes for feeling like an outcast.

The bus stop was where the hell with the bullies began.

"Ching Chong?"

Laughter.

"Hey, slanty eyes!" (while they held their eyes back).

"Hey, I saw your middle name—isn't it like 'King Kong'?" (My middle name is Yu-Kang, which is a family name.)

More laughter.

The bus would finally come.

I would then sit with one of what felt like my only friends, MyMy, a Jewish girl, who was also not part of the "cool" crowd.

Then school was relatively fine...until recess. This was when the bullying would sometimes begin again, this time with a new set of kids. This time, the African American girls would start in on bullying me, also for being Chinese. Looking back, I now find the racism from that particular group paradoxical. But at the time, I thought nothing of it. I just wanted it to not be happening.

Once, when my father came to school with me, I remember one of the girls commenting, "Oh, this time she brought a bodyguard!" Interestingly enough, they didn't comment on his being Chinese, just his being my bodyguard.

My thought process at that time never involved fighting back, though I'm not sure why. Perhaps it's because I thought of myself as average and nothing special. I was also terrible at sports, so that didn't help; the kids who were sports superstars were all super popular, of course. They were the "cool" ones.

So, what did I do about the bullying at the time?

Nothing. Nada. Zippo. I just would sit there and say nothing.

When we are presented with situations where we perceive that a harmful event, threat, or attack is imminent, our brains react physiologically by pumping a surge of hormones into our bodies to prepare us and protect us. The result is that most of us do one of three things: fight, flight, or freeze. I believe that in my childhood, my response was to just *freeze.*

I said nothing to the other kids. I said nothing to the teachers. I said nothing to my parents. I said nothing. I wanted to just not make waves.

You have to remember: this was the 1970s. There were no talk shows about bullying. There were no anti-bullying campaigns. My mom certainly wasn't someone I could talk to about it. Her parents were German immigrants, so she came from very stoic people. And my dad, great as he was at taking care of our needs, wasn't Mr. Let's-Talk-About-Our-Feelings either. He was raised in China until he was fifteen years old, and he was in his forties when I was born.

But inside. Inside I knew I was made for more, even though I felt average on the outside. Somewhere deep down there inside, I heard that whisper. It was my soul. Your soul always remembers and knows. Pierre Teilhard de Chardin said, "We are not human beings having a spiritual experience. We are spiritual beings having a human experience. Yet the imprint of bullying was left there. Your physical body always carries your trauma with you.

Many years later, I thought I had scratched out that imprint. I thought I had done my due diligence as a human in progress.

Went to therapy. Got married at nineteen. Had three kids by the age of twenty-two. Got divorced.

Went to meditation classes. Read lots and lots of self-help books.

Tried the self-flagellation and self-destruction path for a while too.

Got remarried. Had another child. More therapy. I've been on Buddhist retreats. I've even studied Kabbalah privately with a rabbi.

Then when I was closing in on age forty, I decided my career needed a radical shift, so I hired a really good business coach and very quickly became one of the top 1 percent of attorneys in the nation.

Life was good. I wrote two bestselling books. I had a really strong circle of friends. I had a good marriage and a nice family.

That little voiceless girl who was bullied on the playground was long gone. Dust in the wind.

Or so I thought.

Then enter a covert passive-aggressive narcissist business partner. Separate from my law practice, only a few short years ago, I decided to go into an entrepreneurial endeavor with this woman, who seemed smart, experienced, and fun. But underneath her veneer was a jealous, vindictive, deeply insecure person, filled with underlying rage.

Unwittingly, I became her target. Within a short time of becoming involved in a business relationship with this person, old imprints in me began to bubble back to the surface again. I found myself transported back to the Chesterbrook Elementary School playground.

Those feelings of not being good enough, of being small and voiceless, were reignited almost like a pilot light that I thought was no longer lit but it turned out had just been dimmed. It was excruciating, frustrating, and maddening all at once.

Toward the end of this relationship, I met with the business coach whom I'd worked with at that point for more than a decade, who is also an expert in human behavior and the brain, and she said to me, "Rebecca, it's not what's happening or what she is doing or saying, it's how it lands for you."

So profound. Put another way, if someone called you a banana, you would obviously laugh it off and think nothing of it, because you know that it has nothing to do with you whatsoever. Obviously, you know you're not a banana.

It's only when you believe that there might be a modicum of truth to what the other person is saying that it bothers you.

This was an *aha* moment. The grown-up version of me then came flooding back. It was at that moment that my partner's behavior stopped bothering me.

But before I had that *aha* moment, I had found out that this person was a narcissist and had decided to read dozens of books on the topic. I then realized that I had been dealing with narcissists all wrong in my law practice.

I had been litigating high net worth cases for years. I had represented billionaires and celebrities. I had lots and lots of accolades. I had written a bestselling divorce book. But I didn't know anything about narcissism. In the legal world, the term "narcissist" is a fairly new word that's being thrown around. For many years, it seemed like all the wives would say that their husbands were "controlling," and all the husbands would characterize their wives as "crazy." But in the last couple of years, all the parties (on both sides of the cases) have started to use the term "narcissist." This means that judges and attorneys are just now hearing this term regularly. Whether the judges, attorneys, mediators, arbitrators, or others in the court system know what it actually means is another whole conversation.

I will be sharing much more of my own story as I go through the book.

Many narcissists are just grown-up bullies. That's about as plainly as it can be put.

The problem is that the world is overrun with them right now. Experts estimate that potentially up to 15 percent of the world's population either has narcissistic personality disorder, possesses narcissistic traits or tendencies, or has other types of antisocial personality disorders which cause people to lack empathy.

To put that into perspective, there are approximately 7.9 billion people on the planet currently and about 333 million in the United States. If each person in that 15 percent of the population emotionally abuses just three people in their lifetime, that results in approximately 3.4 billion people in the world or 150 million in the United States being the victims of a toxic personality. This is probably why so many of us feel impacted by narcissistic people or people who have these traits or tendencies.

Now, here's the big problem, and here's what I know for sure, sure, sure.

When it comes to communicating or negotiating with narcissists, or litigating with narcissists, we have been going about it *all wrong*.

Narcissists do not think like non-narcissistic people. Their brains do not function in the same way that the rest of the world's brains do, so you cannot interact, negotiate, or deal with them in the same way. If you do, you will fail, and miserably. Every single time. It will cause you searing pain. It will cost you lots of money. It will eventually drain your life and your soul from you. All while the narcissist sits back and enjoys the show, eating their popcorn, watching you slowly becoming a shell of yourself.

I cannot stress this enough.

That's the bad news.

Here's the good news.

Narcissists, while sometimes challenging to deal with, are actually quite predictable in their behavior and extremely easy to read. They do follow patterns. This is how I was able to develop my SLAY Method® and know that, when followed precisely, it absolutely works, so that you can win, every single time. You may have your narcissist asking to resolve issues with you—begging, even.

I know that you picked up this book because you're probably feeling powerless, maybe used and abused, paranoid, or like you're walking on eggshells all the time.

Deep within you, though, the real you—your soul—knows you were born for more, and that is the voice inside yourself that you need to listen to now.

The narcissist just represents the battle to be won. This is a test. A test of your strength.

Whether you have a real trial to go through against them (which I will show you how to win) or a proverbial trial (you will see how to beat that too), once you see how strong you are, you will be able to conquer anything and anyone.

You are on this planet for a reason. You are meant to shine. You are meant to create. You are meant to share your gifts with the world.

Step-by-step, this guidance will show you the way, and I am here to support you in breaking through and breaking free from toxic relationships so that you can shine your light.

Today is a great day to start negotiating your best life.

Now, let's SLAY this!

Rebecca

CHAPTER 1
WELCOME TO HELL

"The path to paradise begins in hell."
DANTE ALIGHIERI, *THE DIVINE COMEDY*

Let's start off by having you think about a time in your life when you were in any type of a relationship, business or personal.

The relationship I want you to think about is a relationship with a person where the person started off being super charming, charismatic, and personable. They seemed absolutely perfect... at first.

It was as though the stars had aligned. If it was a business relationship, they may have had every single skill set you had ever wanted in a business partnership, plus all the most incredible contacts. If they were a potential romantic partner, well, they rocked your world. They were probably intoxicating. You could barely see straight.

This person was so captivating that you were immediately drawn to them.

Another reason you were drawn to them was that they didn't stop communicating with you in the beginning. They had a way of making you feel like you were special—as if you were the most incredible human they had ever met on the planet. You found yourself thinking, *Where has this person been all my life? Wow! They are amazing!*

Then they wanted to hurry the relationship along. Again—this is business or personal. Whatever the next level was, they wanted to get to it—right away. If it was business, they wanted to sign contracts or form a partnership. If it was a romantic relationship, they wanted to meet the family, move in together, and get married—right away. Their philosophy was, "Why wait? We are perfect for each other! Come on. Let's do this now!"

While you may have had some misgivings, or you weren't sure, they talked you into it, overpowered you, and then you found yourself on that next level. Locked in.

Then almost right away…you began to see red flags. You started to see inconsistencies in their stories. Or they would promise to do things but then didn't follow through. Or suddenly they weren't texting you back right away anymore. Or maybe you even caught them in lies.

But they always seemed to have some sort of explanation: it was someone else's fault. Or something was going on in their personal lives. Or maybe it was *your fault*.

Suddenly now, *you* were the issue.

You were too needy. *You* were the one to blame for their problems.

Maybe you asked them about something that they were doing with their friends on a weekend, or something for the business that needed to be discussed. They might have said, "We talked about that, and you agreed; don't you remember?" and you *knew* that conversation never took place.

Perhaps then it started to become confusing for you, because you found yourself wondering what happened to that incredibly charming and charismatic person who initially swept you off your feet.

Then maybe you even started to feel like this person was having conversations about you behind your back with third parties. Perhaps you even read some of their texts or emails that seemed questionable, but when you asked the person about them, they told you that you were crazy, that you were reading too much into them, or that you were jealous or oversensitive.

At some point in that relationship, you might have started to feel disempowered. Your gut might have started to tell you that something was off, but you were already deep into the relationship by that point, so you weren't sure what to do. You might have even started to rationalize with yourself, telling yourself it wasn't always bad and that sometimes the person could be great. You might have found that you were starting to doubt yourself, but you still wondered whether you should trust the other person or not.

You found yourself waking up in the middle of the night thinking about it, waking up in the morning thinking about it, thinking about it when you were brushing your teeth.

In short, you started to obsess about it. Maybe you even started to feel paranoid.

You really started to feel crazy, because a lot of the time, other people thought that other person was absolutely wonderful, which just compounded your feelings of confusion.

You began to feel like something was wrong with you.

You even felt like the person had started to eat away at your soul.

You probably felt like that person was slowly draining the life out of you.

If you have ever experienced that type of a relationship, chances are you've been in a relationship with a narcissist.

I've been there too.

Welcome to the *Hell Club*.

First, I want to acknowledge those of you who have been in relationships with narcissists and managed to escape. That took a hell of a lot of courage and was probably the hardest thing you ever did in your life.

Second, I want to tell you this. I am an attorney who trains people on how to negotiate with narcissists. Yes, I can sit here and tell you all about how I've represented billionaires and celebrities, and that's how I've learned a helluva lot about narcissists and how to negotiate with them.

Period. Hard stop. That is the absolute truth.

I definitely learned a lot about how to negotiate with narcissists from that. But that's not the *only* place I learned about it—and that's *not* my "why."

It was actually just over two years ago that I started making some YouTube videos on negotiation (in general). I was receiving a whopping thirty views a video or so, and I'm *pretty* sure all the views were from my mom and her church friends.

Then I did one video on "How to Negotiate with a Narcissist." All of a sudden that one video got close to seven hundred views!

Now I had a conundrum. I knew that if I wanted to continue to see more hits on my videos on YouTube, I would have to make more content on narcissism and negotiation.

I remember lamenting to my husband in our living room, "I really don't know if I want to be known as the Narcissism Queen!"

He said something about riding the wave and helping people, and to just go with it. So, I kept making videos on the topic, thinking of it in terms of a few more at a time, then a few more, which turned into a few more.

Now, why was I able to speak with such authenticity about how to negotiate with a narcissist?

Well, because, as I mentioned in the preface of this book, a few years before that, I entered into a business endeavor, separate from my law practice, with someone who turned out to be a narcissist.

That business partnership caused me to feel a tremendous amount of angst.

That business partnership caused me to feel massive amounts of anxiety.

That business partnership sent me into this tailspin, which ultimately caused me to dive into reading every book I could get my hands on, on the topic of narcissism.

Now, about the topic of *negotiation*, I had already lectured all over the country, including as a keynote speaker at the American Bar Association. In fact, I was considered an expert in the field already and had been teaching and lecturing on it for nearly two decades. I have a book on it, *Negotiate Like You M.A.T.T.E.R.: The Sure-Fire Method to Step Up and Win*, and Robert Shapiro even wrote the foreword for that book.

But, to paraphrase Ruth Langmore in *Ozark*, I didn't know sh★t about f★ck when it came to *narcissism*. Until I was dealing with a narcissist on a personal level and was thrust into the depths of what that personal hell actually meant, I didn't actually start researching the topic.

I *thought* I knew what a narcissist was, but I didn't. I had participated in hundreds of negotiations and mediations, including many with narcissistic personalities, as an attorney, sometimes representing them and sometimes on the other side. I thought I had been managing them, communicating with them, and negotiating with them in the most optimal way possible, but after really diving into learning about their personalities, I realized I had not.

So, after curling up with my nose in hundreds of books and watching thousands of hours of YouTube videos, I learned quickly. I really wasn't planning to use my knowledge for anything or anyone but myself. I just wanted to learn.

Then, an *aha* moment came to me. A realization. I was still practicing law at the time, and I thought maybe I could take what I was learning and apply it to the cases I had. Perhaps I could see if I could get some of these narcissistic personalities to start to want to resolve the issues.

Eureka! It was as if I had discovered penicillin! Seriously. All of a sudden, I saw movement in these cases.

Then COVID-19 happened, and I couldn't practice law for a while, so I focused on YouTube.

That's when I started doing the videos on how to negotiate with narcissists. It turned out that there was a huge black hole in resources on this topic and a desperate need for information.

So here I am, just over two years later. As of this writing, I have more than 25 million views on YouTube, and I have sold my *SLAY Your Negotiation with a Narcissist* program to thousands of people around the world, in nearly every country, on every continent, and in every state in the United States. Why? Just because there is a need? Partially, yes.

But also because people know that I've been there too.

I'm going to share more of the specifics of my story in dealing with that narcissistic business partner as I go through my SLAY Method® throughout this book. But, more importantly, I want to share this with you right now. I believe that everything in my life has led me on this path to doing what I am doing now.

Having to deal with that person, where I lay awake at night thinking I was going crazy, then woke up in the morning obsessing about it.

Brushing my teeth and feeling paranoid. Feeling that tightness in my chest. Feeling sick to my stomach. Like I had no air. Couldn't breathe.

Honestly, initially, I really didn't want to share my own story of having to deal with a narcissist, because I was supposed to be strong. I was supposed to be this badass attorney!

I was thinking, *How the hell did this happen to me?*

But then I realized that instead of asking that question, I needed to ask myself a different question: *Why did this happen* for *me?*

I needed to get over the blame and shame and just start talking about it.

I needed to be authentic and tell people about it. Not just for other people, but for me and my own healing.

I realized that maybe everything in my life had led me to doing what I am doing now. Wayne Dyer used to say, "When you change the way you look at things, the things you look at change."

Now, I believe I have been chosen by my Creator to be a voice. I believe I am simply the vessel.

While I'm not quite at the point where I can say I'm glad it happened to me, because it was still awful, I do practice gratitude for it. I do believe that it happened for a reason.

Now I'm on a mission—for all people to negotiate their way out of toxic situations and relationships and into their best lives.

Now, Who or What Is a Narcissist?

I'm going to go into much more in depth in Chapter 2, but I want to give you a brief overview here of who this person is.

I want you to picture a person who is totally and completely empty inside. I have often said that narcissists are like those hollow chocolate Easter bunnies. You know, the ones that look pretty on the outside but have nothing inside. Narcissists *feel* like they have no value inside. I say they feel that way, because all humans are inherently very valuable, but because narcissists feel no internal sense of value, they must extrapolate all of their validation from external sources constantly.

This means they are in constant survival mode. It's almost as if they are starving or gasping for breath. They're desperate to survive. In fact, they're so desperate, they can't see you or feel anything about you.

This is why narcissists have no empathy. Think about it. If you were lost on a mountaintop because of an avalanche with someone else, your survival was at stake, and the only thing left to eat was one tiny protein bar, you and the person would likely fight over it to survive. This is how a narcissist feels all the time, and it's why they can't feel anything about you.

The emptiness inside of them is like a black hole. They desperately want you to fill it. In fact, you might want to fill it too. But it cannot be filled, because they are incapable of receiving any sort of true love. Inside, the self-loathing runs deep. They simply lack any self-esteem at all.

This is why, if you're in a relationship with a narcissist, you are left depleted, yet they're still starving. All. The. Time. This is a constant cycle, until it literally feels like a reverse IV has been hooked up to you and all the life has been sucked from your body.

And. It. Cannot. Be. Fixed. (Not easily, anyway.)

It is a scarcity mindset or way of thinking—to the utmost extreme.

Can You Actually Negotiate with a Narcissist? Why Bother to Try?

Most of us recoil just hearing the word narcissist, which brings me to the name of this book: *SLAY the Bully: How to Negotiate with a Narcissist and Win.* Does that sound contradictory to you in some way? Like, *Wait, what?* Everyone knows there's no negotiating with narcissists, right? Why even try, right?

Here's what I know. It's absolutely worth trying, *because narcissists are actually way more afraid of you than you are of them.*

And after twenty years of representing narcissists, being on the other side of narcissists in lawsuits, dealing with them as clients, and, unfortunately, having to deal with them in my personal life, I have a very deep understanding of the psyche of these individuals, and I've turned that understanding into a framework for getting what you want from them.

Everyone else is telling you that negotiating with narcissists is futile and a total waste of time. That you can't win.

I'm telling you that you can win. That with the right negotiation framework and the right understanding of how narcissists think, you can absolutely win. Every single time.

I know firsthand the drama, trauma, and chaos narcissists cause.

In this book, I'm going to give you my framework for slaying your negotiation with the narcissist, so that by the time you are finished reading, you'll know how to shift the narrative, shift the conversation, and shift the dynamic of power, so that you feel more confident and empowered in every aspect of your life.

While my experience has been in the legal field, I am here to help you deal with toxic people in your everyday lives. If you are dealing with a family member, a bully in the workplace, a toxic neighbor, an intimidating boss or client, a crazy ex or co-parent, or any kind of situation where you want to be able to communicate or negotiate from a more powerful place, then this book is for you. This framework will apply across the board in all situations. If you are dealing with human beings in any country, in any language, then these methodologies will work.

SLAY Method® at a Glance

Narcissists love to trigger you. They love to manipulate you. They love to see you squirm, so if you are *negotiating* with them and you try to deal with them like you would non-narcissistic people, you absolutely will fail. You will fail 100 percent of the time.

This means you absolutely must have a framework. It's the only way. I've had clients who had been dealing with narcissists for years, paralyzed in fear, and they grabbed onto this framework like a lifeline, and within a few weeks, they snapped the narcissist into place like a rubber band. It's incredible.

Here is an overview of the SLAY Your Negotiation with a Narcissist framework, which we will go into much more detail in as we go through the book.

S stands for **Strategy**. This is where you will create your Super Strong Strategy. This will provide the framework for your entire negotiation and be your North Star throughout the process. This is almost like the GPS in your car. You begin with the end in mind. Here, you will create your Vision. Then you will create action steps and do your research, but so many times when you're dealing with narcissists, you get so caught up in defending yourself that you forget to think about what it is that you actually want out of the negotiation. You're like a turtle on your back! But if you don't figure out what you want from the narcissist, then you can't get it. There will be several steps to this process, and this is where you will begin to turn it all around so that you are no longer feeling paralyzed, used, and abused.

L stands for **Leverage**. This is where you will motivate and incentivize the narcissist to want to come to a peaceful resolution with you by understanding what makes them tick. Narcissists are motivated by the same things as healthy people, but they don't think like non-narcissistic people, so you *cannot negotiate with them like you do non-narcissistic people.* Period. If you create an invisible fence around the narcissist and do this the right way, by creating a smart strategy and then applying the right leverage, you can have the narcissist begging you to resolve your negotiation.

A stands for **Anticipate**. This is where you get two steps ahead of the narcissist in anticipating their behavior, their arguments, and what is motivating them. In this section, you will not only be able to predict the types of narcissists that you are dealing with and the way that they actually behave in negotiation (yes, they are different), but also in this chapter, I will offer many different ways to actually respond, stay calm, master your emotions, and—most important—*not take the narcissist's bait*, so that you don't get sucked into their mud. You will also know exactly what games to anticipate that they will play, so that you can shut them down before they start.

Y stands for **You** and **Your position**. There are really two elements to this part of the framework.

The first part of You is *tactical.* You must understand that you have to think offensively. The best football teams don't win because all they had was a great defense. Baseball teams don't win because their outfield guys are killer. No. Football teams win because their offense scores points. Baseball teams win because they have batters that hit the ball out of the park. In short, they have a great offense. Well, I could go on and on here. But I will save it for the chapter.

The second part ofYou is *mental.* Mindset is everything—90 percent of winning has begins before you even walk into the room. If you don't believe you can win, ain't nobody can help you. If you think you're always going to be a victim and that's that, you can just put this book down right now, or if you're listening to the audio version, just shut it off and walk away. This is not the book for you.

But if you do believe, then that's what the second part of the Y is about: focusing on *you.*

Hey, listen: you don't have to be all in just yet. In fact, you can think, *Well,* maybe *it's possible.* Or even *I want to believe it's possible.* That's okay too. As long as there's some little kernel of light in there that believes it can happen, that's where we start. This section is where I work with you and your mindset, to help you shift your thinking.

On my website at www.slaythebully.com/resources I have a free SLAY chart for you that will remind you what each of these stands for: S-L-A-Y. SLAY. I want you to print that chart out and put it somewhere where you can see it every single day, especially as we are going through each of the chapters of this book.

Getting Out of Hell

Dealing with a narcissistic business partner was one of the worst, most heinous situations of my life. When I tried to get out of it, this person made it extremely difficult for me.

I'm going to go into this more in the next chapter, but staying in a relationship with a narcissist just is really and truly not an option. They generally do not change. The business partner I had a relationship with tried to get better once she realized that I was pulling back, but then once she realized that I definitely was no longer interested in remaining in the partnership, she became far worse than even I could have imagined. This actually only served to validate my decision to leave that partnership, but it didn't make it easier. My point, though, is that she hadn't actually "changed."

I have interviewed many psychiatrists and psychologists, and they have said that narcissists, for the most part, do not change their behavior. In fact, some of the mental health experts I interviewed even went as far as to say that they will not even treat narcissists because they cannot be rehabilitated.

The reason it is so difficult for mental health specialists to treat people with narcissism is because of the very nature of the disorder itself. People with narcissism don't tend to be people who want to sit around and ponder their faults and flaws. Criticism to a narcissist is like sunlight to a vampire. Or at least they feel like it's fatal anyway. It's the last thing they want.

I've always loved the movie *The Wizard of Oz*. Now, looking back, I see how the Great and Powerful Oz was a lot like the narcissist: behind the curtain was really a feeble, scared, little man. Dorothy, the Scarecrow, the Tin Man, and the Cowardly Lion all thought the Wizard was the one who knew everything and could give them everything they wanted, until they figured out that they had to take the journey to finding themselves all along. At the end of the movie, Dorothy had to tap her red shoes together to find her way home, back to her true self.

The SLAY Method® gives you the strategy to pull back the curtain, or threaten to pull it back, so that the narcissist feels exposed, while you find your courage, your heart, and your home along the way.

It's all so exciting! I can't wait to show you the way. In Chapter 2, we're going to dig deep into why your soul is screaming for help right now, and how we can throw it a lifeline.

Ready? Awesome. Let's tap our red shoes together and get this party started!

What You Can Do Now to Start SLAYing

- **Stop**
    - Blaming yourself
    - Feeling guilty
    - Getting into the mud with the narcissist
    - Allowing the narcissist to trigger you

- **Start**
    - Realizing the 3 Cs: you didn't Cause it ("it" meaning the situation with the narcissist, anything the narcissist does to you, or how the narcissist treats you), you can't Control it, and you can't Control the narcissist
    - Knowing that you are in the right place and that you picked this book up for a reason
    - Believing that on the other side of the greatest suffering awaits your greatest self
    - Going to www.slaythebully.com/resources, grabbing your free SLAY chart, putting it somewhere where you'll be able to see it every single day, and knowing that you CAN win!

Mantra for Today:

Today *is a great day to start negotiating my best life.*
(Or write one of your own that speaks to you….)

CHAPTER 2
YOUR SOUL'S SCREAM FOR HELP

"You can't swing a cat without hitting a narcissist."
Brené Brown

"It's time to either end the marriage or end my life," she murmured to me.

While she looked composed, her spirit was on fumes. Gone.

What other kinds of things was she saying after having been married for more than three decades?

"Am I going crazy?"

"How the hell did I end up in this position?"

"Deep down, he's actually not a bad guy. He lashes out. He can't help himself. But I can't take it anymore."

She started to sob. Then she said these words: "Help me please. I need to figure out *how to escape*."

How to *escape*.

Were we planning a prison bust? An attempted escape from terrorist captors? Well, not the kind you might traditionally think of.

This conversation occurred during an initial client meeting in my office. Lorretta found herself broken, scared to death for her future, and beaten down from years living with a man who had her convinced that not only was she totally crazy, but that if she left him, he would make good on his promise to make her life a living hell. But after years of being berated, derided, and emotionally abused, she realized she just couldn't go on in the relationship.

She decided her freedom was worth the risk of what he might do.

An attractive woman in her fifties, she had two adult daughters whom she loved more than life. When her kids were little, she was too afraid to leave them with him.

Lorretta's family of origin was a family of professionals: her two brothers were both physicians, and her father had been a successful entrepreneur. She had parents who were loving, supportive, and lived nearby. Her brothers and parents had also given her money toward her attorney's fees.

She and her husband had also done well for themselves. They had started a couple of businesses, both of which had flourished. They had a couple of very nice homes and a few cars, and their girls had attended one of the local private schools.

Now, does this seem like a person who would *contemplate suicide*?

Probably not.

When people leave narcissistic relationships—business or personal—they don't casually pack their things or nonchalantly walk out the door. They don't peacefully say goodbyes or wish each other well. No. Quite the contrary. They generally run like hell from the relationship, screaming as if their hair has been set on fire, or they sneak out in the middle of the night as if they are carrying out a covert operation more secretive than one planned by a Navy SEAL team.

In other words, when people leave relationships with narcissists, regardless of whether the relationship has been business or personal, they feel like they desperately need to *escape* from the relationships to *save their souls*.

In fact, Lorretta had tried to leave once before, and then ended up reconciling with her husband, because she hadn't properly "planned." She didn't have enough money to live on her own, and her husband terrorized her. At first. Then he begged. Then he guilted her into returning and said he would do "anything" to get her back.

When she returned, he pretended to be different at first. He went along with counseling and said he had "changed." Then eventually she realized it was all a manipulation, and Dr. Jekyll quickly turned back into Mr. Hyde again. But the next time she left, she formulated a plan. She waited until he was asleep, then packed her things, snuck out in the middle of the night, and went to her mother's home. She had already hired me, and we had already filed the petition for dissolution of marriage, and that document, along with all the documents to be served upon "Mr. Wonderful," were already in the hands of the process server.

We just needed to give the process server the go ahead. Once she was safely ensconced at her mom's, we gave the process server the date and time to be served, along with the address and a picture of him, and bam! He was served.

At first, he didn't know where she was. But once he found out she had been hiding at her mother's home, he showed up there. He began banging on the doors and windows, screaming and yelling, causing a horrible scene, and saying that she needed to return home. He accused her of abandoning the family and their businesses and called her despicable names. He then blew up her phone with text messages attempting to guilt her into coming back.

When that didn't work, he took it up a level, going to the next trigger point for her. He moved on to threatening the employees of the businesses. But he couldn't just make a normal threat. That wouldn't be enough to draw her back in. Because she was managing the businesses, *and* because he knew how much she deeply cared about the employees, he physically went after one of them.

Being a construction business, it was that kind of environment where there were tough guys coming in and out of the office all the time, but it was a large business. They had about thirty trucks and dozens of employees, with a lot of job sites. There was a lot at stake, and he knew it. She had been the one holding it all together.

Then he proceeded to threaten to burn it all to the ground. Yes, he threatened to burn his own entire business to the ground, just to hurt her.

Does this story sound dramatic? Think I'm puffing this story up to make it seem crazier for this book? Do you think narcissists only act like this in domestic situations?

Sadly, the answers to these questions are: nope. Nope. And um, *nope*.

Now, at this juncture, before we go much deeper here, this is a good time to define what a narcissist actually is.

What Is a Narcissist?

A narcissist has no sense of self, and because of this, they loathe criticism, are extremely jealous and small-minded, want everyone to view them as "special," and manipulate people for their own gain, without regard for other people's feelings or the consequences of their own behaviors. True narcissism is a legitimate personality disorder that is rarely, if ever, cured.

We hear about narcissists all the time in the media nowadays, it seems, and in all different forums, but we don't really know what the word actually means. Without diving into the details of these stories, here are just some examples of headlines that we've heard in the news in different forums.

During the Johnny Depp and Amber Heard trial, *both* were accused of being narcissists, although the court of public opinion overwhelmingly decided that *she* was clearly the bigger *narcissist.*

When Britney Spears was trying to break free of the chains of her father's conservatorship, what did the court of public opinion decide her father was? A *narcissist.*

The sports world went crazy when Jimbo Fisher, one of the biggest names in college football coaching, called Nick Saban, another hugely popular coach, a *narcissist.*

With all this talk about narcissists, it is important that we know what a narcissist actually is, but I think it is even more critical that we know how to communicate with them, how to manage them, and how to *negotiate with them.*

Sometimes people wonder, *Is this person a narcissist? Or are they just a jackass?* The sad truth is that we are less likely to notice a narcissist when we see one because narcissists often hide in plain sight behind their charm and charisma, and then only actually act like jackasses to those whom they have "targeted" behind closed doors.

We find ourselves in unfortunate situations, losing reasonable negotiations, ready to give up, and only asking ourselves, "How did I get here?" once it's too late (meaning you're already in the relationship because they've love bombed you and you're drowning at that point). But regardless of how you ended up at the "destination" (sometimes also referred to as Satan's living room or Dante's eighth concentric circle of hell), know this: a jackass, while no picnic to deal with, has moments when they have lapses in their behavior, but they can be corrected and can actually feel remorse, whereas a narcissist rarely, if ever, feels any remorse.

The word narcissism comes from the story of Narcissus. Narcissus was a young man who, according to Greek mythology, was quite handsome. People would swoon and fall for him immediately upon seeing him, but he treated them with total disdain. One of those young beauties was a nymph named Echo. He totally broke her heart, so he was cursed to live a life of unrequited love forever. The story goes that one day he was hunting in the woods, and he caught a glimpse of himself in a pool of water and fell in love with himself. He knelt to try to kiss his reflection, but of course he couldn't catch it, and he fell in and drowned. In his place, the beautiful narcissus flower appeared instead.

There are a few great lessons to be learned from young Narcissus, which we will see play out here in this book. One is that he was totally unable to truly connect with others. The second is that he never knew true and authentic love. The third is that he had no empathy for others and, most importantly, was unable to see how that path of destruction would ultimately lead to his downfall. That is what very often happens with narcissists.

Mental health professionals use The American Psychiatric Association's *Diagnostic and Statistical Manual of Mental Disorders, Fifth Edition (DSM-5-TR)* to determine if someone has narcissistic personality disorder (NPD). It's a somewhat subjective test, in which the experts are to take a look at nine different criteria, for an adult subject, and determine if the subject in question meets at least five of the nine criteria. The nine criteria outline the following factors:

1. *Here, the DSM-5-TR refers to* ***grandiosity and exaggeration****. This factor would be best associated with the grandiose narcissist, who tells everyone how great they are, and in fact*

probably isn't truthful about their achievements. The goal and objective is to look as good as possible so that everyone in their world will fawn and adulate all over them as much as possible.

2. *This factor refers to an obsession with being* ***powerful, beautiful*** *or achieving* ***unlimited success****. The DSM-5-TR uses the word "****preoccupied****," but it really is more like an obsession with a narcissist—to the detriment of others and even themselves.*
3. *Next, the narcissist desires to feel not only that they are "****special****" but that they should have* ***special treatment****. Again, to the detriment of others. No one else gets the best table at that restaurant. No one else should have that amazing dress.*
4. *In this factor, the DSM-5-TR lists a narcissist's deep-seated need for* ***constant and "excessive admiration."*** *Everyone loves a compliment. Who doesn't love to be flattered? This is beyond that. Narcissists desperately crave it, often to the detriment of others, and again, it can be an obsession.*
5. *This factor asks the practitioner to look at whether the person believes they are entitled to special privileges or treatment. Narcissists often demand particularly favorable treatment and failure to comply can be considered a personal slight to them. This can open Pandora's Box. Their ego (narcissistic injury) is bruised, which means that narcissistic rage can come flying out.*
6. *Next, the DSM-5-TR considers whether the person regularly* ***exploits*** *people or* ***uses them for their own gain****. Are their relationships completely transactional—meaning that they don't do anything for someone unless there is something in it for them? Many times, narcissists use people just for what they need for themselves with regard for the other person's feelings or interests and then when they've gotten what they needed out*

of the relationship, they like cow's cud, they've chewed them up, spit them out, and on they go. No looking back.

7. *Here, the mental health practitioner will also have to determine whether or not the person has the ability to feel* ***true empathy*** *for others. This is a biggie of course. Discovering whether a person actually feels true care about the feelings and needs of another is probably the most important part of this assessment. (The skeptic in me does wonder how accurate these assessments can be at measuring true empathy.)*
8. *This factor considers whether the narcissist is* ***jealous of others or thinks others are of him or her****. Now, of course, we have all been jealous at some point in our lives. We wouldn't be human if we hadn't. But narcissists set up permanent homes, and live there for good. They never leave there. It's their every day. Not only are they* ***jealous of anyone else*** *that they think has anything that they perceive has more, better, higher, or anything they think they should have; they are also genuinely believe others who less than they do are* ***jealous of them****. Furthermore, this insane game continues with them deeply wanting anyone they perceive to* ***be or have less than do*** *to be* ***jealous of them****. It's an exhausting existence.*
9. *Finally, in this last factor, the practitioner has to determine how* ***arrogant*** *the person is. Remember the arrogance is really a charade. Narcissists who are low on supply may "reinflate" their own self-importance by degrading others.*

In June 2011, the American Psychiatric Association revised the criteria to actually diagnose a person with NPD, to add even more criteria with regard to empathy, entitlement, exploitation, condescending behaviors, attention-seeking behaviors, grandiose fantasies, and more. It does specifically state that NPD is a "pathological" state and not due to physiological issues, such as drug abuse or head traumas, for example.

Thus, narcissism is a real disorder that can be evaluated. But read on for the potential issues in knowing the actual number of people afflicted with narcissism.

Narcissism by the Numbers

Bear in mind that people who are actually *diagnosed* with NPD represent the furthest end of the spectrum. Also bear in mind that people who actually have NPD are the *least likely* of the people who have issues with mental health to walk into a mental health professional's office to be evaluated. Thus, there are likely a lot more narcissists walking around than we realize.

Without getting too deep into the weeds here, as I briefly touched upon earlier, the DSM-5-TR estimates that approximately 15 percent of the population has some type of personality disorder in which the person diagnosed would tend to lack empathy in some way (which include narcissism, antisocial personality disorders, and others.) In his book, *Splitting: Protecting Yourself While Divorcing Someone with Borderline or Narcissistic Personality Disorder*, Bill Eddy did a deep dive into the statistics and made some interesting finds. The statistics over the last two decades are indicating a rapid increase in narcissism, especially in younger age groups. He also found that, while there are more male narcissists than female, narcissistic women can also be "very harmful." I can certainly attest to having seen that in my own law practice as well.

Finally, I think it is very important to note that the DSM-5-TR estimates are the *extremes*. Those estimates leave out people who might simply have narcissistic traits or tendencies but can still make people's lives pretty darn miserable.

I also want to point out an observation of my own. In my area of practice, high net worth divorce, when I was practicing regularly, we were able to regularly settle approximately 85 percent of our cases. The other 15 percent would always have to go to trial. I didn't know about narcissism at the time when I was practicing full time, but I did know that when cases didn't settle, it was almost always because one or both of the parties were just ridiculously unreasonable (or their lawyers were).

Now, taking a look at the DSM-5-TR statistics for personality disorders, which is 15 percent of the population, and aligning that percentage of divorce cases that *do not settle*, which is also 15 percent of the population, I do not think that is a coincidence. I believe it is precisely those people who have personality disorders on one or both sides of those cases; that 15 percent of the population largely makes up the 15 percent of people who end up not settling their cases, then proceeding to trial. Why? Because they enjoy the process of watching the other person squirm.

I want to make some distinctions here. First is that all people want to feel seen and heard and know that they matter. To feel that way doesn't make you a narcissist; that just makes you a human. Second, being confident in yourself doesn't make you a narcissist. Again, you should be confident in yourself. Having self-esteem is a good thing.

Self-esteem is an internal feeling of self-respect. This is that feeling of self-worth and internal value that the narcissist lacks. To assert your accomplishments, for example, and be proud of them, does not make you a narcissist. The question is whether you have feelings of empathy for others.

Dr. Craig Malkin, in his book *Rethinking Narcissism: The Secret to Recognizing and Coping with Narcissists*, shared that narcissism exists on a spectrum, and further that there is a "dark triad" of narcissism. The first part of the triad is the narcissist's dependency on feeling special—and being the *only* one who gets to feel special—the second part is their lack of remorse for how they treat others, and the third part is a penchant for manipulation. Quite the fun little combo.

Where Does Narcissism Come From?

Science tells us that it's definitely nurture and not nature. This means people aren't born with it. All the resources and practitioners seem to conclude that it stems from the narcissist's needs not being properly met in childhood due to trauma, neglect, or even overindulgence.

Dr. Drew Pinsky explained the genesis of narcissism in his book *The Mirror Effect: How Celebrity Narcissism Is Seducing America.* As infants, we are purely focused on survival and having our needs met. During our formative years, we are expected to form healthy connections and secure attachments. Secure attachments are critical for emotional regulation and for developing feelings of empathy.

If that secure attachment doesn't happen, then these children come to rely on what he explains is a form of "dissociation," which causes the fight, flight, or freeze response in them. This dissociation is connected to trauma and is the brain's way of protecting us from terror. In that moment, we actually cut ourselves away from reality as a method of escaping the pain. Dr. Drew explained that the many instances of trauma cause narcissists' brains to actually become bathed in the hormones over and over again, which prepare them for an assault, which leads to an emotional retardation in the development of their brains. That then in turn lays the foundation for the development of narcissistic personality disorder.

Narcissists really are toddlers stuck in adult bodies. But here's the thing: living day to day is always all about survival for them. Here's why.

Narcissism is All About "Survival of the Fittest"

Because the narcissists didn't have their needs met as children, they decided that they had to do what they needed to do to "survive" and to not get "hurt." They were exposed to complex trauma during their development years in childhood, and thus their limbic brain—the part of the brain that is involved with emotion and survival (the "fight, flight, or freeze" portion)—took over. They didn't feel secure and loved, but rather like they had to do what was needed to "survive."

In other words, a shift in priorities took place as a child. For some children, it is subtle, so they just have some narcissistic tendencies, but others become full-blown, pure narcissists.

Narcissistic Injury

The majority of children who grow up in homes where they were exposed to traumatic situations don't become full narcissists. Remember there is a spectrum. Dr. Malkin even identifies a form of healthy narcissism (part of a spectrum of self-enhancement, which he describes as a slightly overly positive and unrealistic view of self). But into adulthood, even people who aren't full narcissists can have narcissistic traits, including the same fight, flight, or freeze response described by Dr. Drew.

During their regular day-to-day life, narcissists function somewhat normally. The cerebral cortex section of their brains takes over. This is the part of the brain responsible for planning, self-control, and judgment. But depending upon the circumstances and, more importantly, the stimuli, the limbic brain becomes activated, then immediately takes over again. Examples of circumstances that might cause this to happen could be when the narcissist feels slighted or disrespected in any way, if they get caught doing something they shouldn't, if they aren't the center of attention when they think they should be, if they sense of loss of control, or if they are exposed.

Narcissistic injury, sometimes referred to as narcissistic shame or a narcissistic wound, refers to an area or areas of trauma or scars that when touched upon can cause a narcissist to immediately lash out or cause their self-defense mechanisms to be triggered. Their self-defense mechanisms are usually not in line with what a rational person believes a normal response would be to the stimuli.

I have often said that narcissists are very easily slighted. I even joke sometimes that you have to watch your tone with narcissists and not use even a little bit of sarcasm, because they hear tones like dogs hear whistles. Even if there's no tone at all, they hear tone. This is why: they are extremely sensitive.

This is just the tip of the iceberg of beginning to understand why you can't negotiate with narcissists as you would with others.

Narcissistic Rage

When that narcissistic injury gets triggered, all hell breaks loose, and narcissistic rage comes flying out. Then the tidal wave comes.

This is when their emotions take over. During this period of time, depending upon the severity of narcissism, the person can go from 0 to 100 immediately. They revert to toddler types of behavior and have tantrums—but in adult forms. In this state, without filters and without boundaries, they can become dangerous at times.

For example, in Lorretta's case, during our first mediation, her husband, a malignant narcissist, showed up without an attorney. He was triggered by our request for support. We went into another room, while he met with the mediator. We could hear him yelling and screaming at the mediator, then he punched the wall and put a hole in it before leaving the office. There was no reasoning with him.

We did eventually get Loretta's case settled. He actually ended up begging her to settle the case because we used the SLAY Method®. As we go through the steps here, remember that you do have to put in the work. There is no magic wand that gives you instant relief. I wish there were.

Narcissistic rage can be triggered by many different things. Narcissists have a deep sense of shame. Brené Brown, in her book *Daring Greatly: How the Courage to Be Vulnerable Transforms the Way We Live, Love, Parent, and Lead*, acknowledged that those of us who've been wronged by narcissists feel like we want to "cut them down to size" and like the "egomaniacs need to know that they're not special, they're not that great, they're not entitled to jack, and they need to get over themselves."

But when we are trying to communicate and negotiate with them in a way that is productive, that definitely will not work. As we get deeper into it here, you will see this is true for several reasons, including, most significantly, that it may trigger their narcissistic rage.

Brown further explains that the underpinning of narcissism is deep shame. She goes on to state that it can't be fixed by simply cutting people down to size and reminding people of how small and inadequate they are. That would just aggravate the problem even more! She has mentioned in many of her talks and her writings that narcissists suffer the most from shame, and that the root cause of their insufferable behavior is that shame.

Narcissists are deeply insecure and have no sense of self. While they may act pretentious and important, it's a huge act slapped onto a person who, underneath it all, feels deeply empty, powerless, and inferior.

This is so critical to understand when dealing with and negotiating with narcissists. How can we possibly negotiate with people who think so differently from us? This does not make rational sense. We absolutely must have a different paradigm in negotiating with them.

The Inherent Problem with the Entire Negotiation System

While I was in law school, in Torts class we had a standard code for a person who was considered "reasonable." In any negligence action, it was a standard that was created for juries, judges, or courts to use to determine objectively if a person's actions constituted negligence. In other words, would a reasonably prudent person act in a certain way when presented with the same set of circumstances? It is a foreseeability test.

In Torts law, this test is also referred to as the "reasonably prudent person" standard. This is defined in general as a practical individual who uses good judgment and common sense in handling matters. I believe that's what judges and lawyers *think* most people in the system are. I believe that's what we all believe most people to be, and I believe that therein lies the inherent problem that we have.

I will refer to what "most people" think of as "reasonable people" or "healthy people" throughout this book, because I believe that we, as humans, instinctively want to measure *all humans* in this way. We try and try and try to apply this sort of "reasonable person" standard to narcissists subconsciously. I see this with clients, and I also do this personally, even though I know, intellectually, I shouldn't. I still catch myself and remind myself of this.

Honestly, for your own sake and your own sanity, it is easier to just assume that they *will not behave* in a manner that is rational. For example, I had a client once, named Amy, who called me from her children's school directly after drop-off in the morning. She had had a run-in with the soon-to-be-ex, Howard, there and was quite emotional. Howard had triggered her big time. All of her sentences began with "Can you believe he did this?" and "Can you believe he said that?" And after empathizing with her, I responded, "Yes, I can. What I can't believe is that you don't believe it! You've been telling me that this is who he has been for the past fifteen years!" And then she laughed and said, "My God, you are absolutely right!"

The Cast of Characters: The Main Types of Narcissists

Narcissists can come in many different types, but there are three main ones that are generally spoken of and that I have chosen to focus upon for negotiation purposes here. Here they are in no particular order.

The first one is the grandiose narcissist (a.k.a. the extraverted narcissist), according to Dr. Malkin. I think of this as your garden variety narcissist. This is the boastful one or bragging one, the one who enters the room and holds court. This person can be male or female but generally skews male. They can be very charismatic to the rest of the world, as all narcissists can be. To be honest, this is the only type of narcissist I ever even knew existed until just a few years ago.

The grandiose narcissist tends to be very dominant and aggressive. You usually don't have any trouble spotting this one. This is the one who is impulsive, who will ignore people's advice, and who is a huge risk taker. These are your CEO types, but the kind who won't bat an eye when it comes to questionable accounting practices. As an attorney, I had a client who was a grandiose narcissist once, who would constantly try to goad me into filing false pleadings, and when I wouldn't, he would say things like, "You're gonna be awfully lonely in heaven, Rebecca." These are the guys (or gals) who tend to be way overconfident in their abilities, probably even when they shouldn't be.

The second main one you hear of often is the covert narcissist or introverted narcissist (this one is also sometimes referred to as the vulnerable narcissist). This one can also be male or female. This one tends to be much more understated and can be humbler. They can often even play the victim or can be found in roles such as pastors or caregivers. They seem like they are the nicest people ever—at first glance, or to people who don't actually know them behind closed doors. I sort of think of the grandiose narcissist as the wolf and the covert narcissist as the wolf in sheep's clothing. This one is much stealthier, more passive-aggressive, and, in a lot of ways, more dangerous, because they are super difficult to spot initially.

The covert narcissist may rush to the side of a person who is in the hospital and stay right by their side the entire time, but it might be an odd display of care, because they may hardly know the person. It will be a strategic move calculated to garner favor for them.

Covert narcissists loooove to play the victim for attention. For example, a female covert narcissist mother may appear to the outside world like a wonderful mother, while purposefully manipulating situations with her adult children behind the scenes, so that when her children do finally reject her, everyone in her outer circle who isn't aware of the real story will view her as the victim. She then does nothing to attempt to repair the relationship with her children, because she would rather appear to be the victim than have the relationship with her family. This is because, as a covert narcissist, the *attention* means more to her.

The last main one is the malignant narcissist. (I think of this one as Darth Vader.) This one can also be male or female and has an overlay of being a sociopath or having antisocial personality disorder. This one has no problemo with ruining your life. The other types of narcissists will hold back at least somewhat, for one reason or another, meaning they know to at least keep themselves looking good on the surface for as long as possible. This one may not. This is a scary narcissist. Definitely steer clear.

So, for example, this is the one who might lie and say that a person is a child molester when they have never touched a child inappropriately or even ever thought of a child in an inappropriate manner. Or this is the one who might become a stalker, threaten violence, or actually carry out acts of violence.

I will elaborate more on each of the types of narcissists and how they behave in negotiations and more importantly, what you should expect from each and how you can handle each in Chapter 7, but for now I wanted to just introduce you to the cast of characters here.

Narcissistic Supply Is the Key to the Narcissist's Kingdom (and Thus Your Freedom)

Okay, so now you know the definition of a narcissist and the main types of narcissists, but what makes a narcissist tick?

While the rest of the world is motivated by many different things, narcissists are motivated by one thing and one thing only: narcissistic supply. They are like rats in a maze. Supply is their cheese. It is their food, their life blood, and their oxygen. It is anything that feeds their ego.

In Chapter 6, we will learn how to use their supply sources as leverage when it comes to negotiating with them, as this is also their Achilles heel. For now, understand that narcissistic supply is what they are after at all times.

Picture animals on the Serengeti constantly scanning and looking for their next source of food. Narcissists' brains are always in scarcity mentality, so they will do anything to protect their supply sources. They will beg, borrow, maim, lie, intimidate, gaslight, threaten, stalk, maybe even kill to protect their sources of supply. It is literally survival to them.

Remember that narcissists' brains were "bathed in chemicals" as children on a regular basis so that they were constantly in survival mode, and so their brains literally do not function in the same way that non-narcissistic people's brains function.

Narcissistic Relationship Phases

The "Love bomb" Phase

Regardless of the *type* of narcissist you are dealing with, they all begin relationships in pretty much the same way. This early phase is often referred to as the "love bombing" stage or the idealization phase. It can last as little as a few months or even up to a year, and it applies to both business and personal relationships.

Narcissists always start off with love bombing, then move into devaluing, and end with discarding, but there is a massive amount of toxic stew in between. So, while you are trying to negotiate with that craziness, it is imperative to have a structure in place or you'll never make it. In Chapter 3, I will focus much more closely on more of the ways narcissists destabilize and weaken you.

During the love bombing phase, the narcissist appears quite charming, charismatic, and captivating. The narcissist is often very smart and well-groomed. Narcissists are quite adept at reading people, as this has been a skill they have had to hone to "survive" since childhood. Malcolm Gladwell, in his bestselling book, *Outliers: The Story of Success*, famously concluded that it takes ten thousand hours of intensive practice to achieve mastery at something that takes skill. Under that theory, even at only three hours per day of practice, one would require only nine years to achieve mastery and to become adept at a particular skill. Well, narcissists have spent their entire lives ensuring that their prowess for reading people is as adroit as possible. They know how to read their targets and become the "perfect" person for you. During this phase, narcissists will often use a technique called *mirroring*, where they will dress like you, talk like you, and even use your mannerisms, so that you find yourself liking them even more.

During the love bombing stage, you will be completely overwhelmed by emotion. This stage can sometimes be characterized by grand gestures such as lavish trips, hundreds of text messages per day, and lots and lots of talk about the future, how incredible you are, and how perfect you are for each other. Again, this is in business or personal relationships.

In my situation, I was taken in by someone who wanted to partner with me for a business relationship. This person talked endlessly about how much we had in common and kept pointing out how much our backgrounds complemented each other for the business I had just set up. She mentioned all the incredible contacts she had and how much she could offer me. She would send me constant emails with lots of ideas to show me how excited she was about my business. She said she was so impressed with me and could get me certain keynote speaking engagements.

During the love bombing phase, narcissists put a lot of pressure on their targets to get to whatever the next level of the relationship is. This is because all of this love bombing is really an investment, and they want to see some major ROI (return on their investment) sooner rather than later. They definitely do *not* want to have to love bomb you any longer than they must. It's all part of the manipulation. They want you to become reliant on them. They want you to think they are incredible and God's gift to you. They want to ensnare and entrap you into their web as fast as possible.

Thus, if the relationship is personal, the narcissist will be pressuring you almost immediately to move in together, let them meet your family, or get married. The narcissist might also even pressure you to cede control of your finances to them and start isolating you from your family and close friends almost immediately. If the relationship is professional, then the narcissist might want to sign contracts right away, enter into a partnership immediately, or something else that causes you to be joined at the hip with this person. If you hesitate at all, the narcissist will talk you into it. "Why wait?" You're perfect for each other! The stars have aligned! This is your moment! And oftentimes, they are so smooth and so beguiling that you find yourself going along, even against your better judgment.

In my case, I did see some red flags, but somehow, I ignored them because her charm overwhelmed me. I thought she seemed so nice. She painted this incredible picture. The narcissist that I dealt with was a covert, passive-aggressive narcissist. I had never seen that type of narcissist before. It wasn't until several months after I had severed the relationship that I even discovered that the person was a narcissist at all. I didn't even realize that narcissists could be female! That's how little I knew about narcissism before this journey started for me a few years ago.

This phase, for the narcissist, is really a grooming phase too. It's a conditioning phase. It's the beginning of the manipulation. They are testing you to see if you will be a good target. Are you an empathic person? Will you provide what their ego needs? Do you have enough value for them in the forms that they are seeking—whatever that might be? They might be seeking money, sex, a place to live, prestige, social climbing, career climbing, looking good (if you are much younger and more attractive), celebrity, or something as simple as constant adulation and compliments.

You have likely seen the love bombing phase played out with celebrities. Kanye West gave us a perfect example of love bombing a few years ago when he publicly gushed about how he surprised and spoiled his new flame, Julia Fox, with an "intimate photo shoot," and he even so generously showered her with an entire hotel suite full of new clothes "that made her feel like Cinderella." He even directed the photo shoot himself. The photoshoot took place in a Michelin star restaurant in New York, which, of course, he had closed that evening just for the two of them. Apparently, the two met in Miami and had an "instant connection," and so they "decided to keep the energy going," so he picked her up in his jet and flew her to New York right away. Of course, he had to write about this entire evening on his blog and make sure that his former wife, Kim Kardashian, knew about every moment of it, so that she would be sufficiently jealous.

As you can see with the Kanye West example above, the love bombing stage is about grooming and about taking control. It's about seeing if you will be of sufficient value to the narcissist for what they need to try to fill that empty void inside of them at that time.

One very important thing to remember about how and why you are chosen: narcissists do not choose you because you have so little value. They choose you because you have so much value. They choose you because of what you can offer them. Narcissists are excellent opportunists. They attach themselves to you because you offer something to them that they want. It is very important to remember this as we go into understanding the devalue phase.

The "Devalue" Phase

Your narcissist has locked you in somehow, as quickly as possible. You have moved into their home, met the family, signed some sort of deal with them, or been hired by them. They want to be sure that you are sufficiently under their spell or control, and once that happens, then the shift happens. This is when their true selves start to show. It's almost as if they have been holding their breath, and they can finally exhale.

This is when you start to see the real red flags. You saw some of them pop up during the love bombing phase when they were moving the relationship along very quickly and coming on strongly. Maybe during the love bombing phase you saw parts of their backstory not totally adding up, but they always had some sort of quick explanation for you. But now you really start to see it.

This is a very confusing time.

This period is marked by hot and cold. You may be insulted either subtly or directly. It may be in front of people or behind closed doors. During this devalue phase, you may also start to see lies and inconsistencies in things that they tell you. Or maybe they will say they are going to do something for you, then not follow through, and if you follow up, then they consider it criticism, it sparks rage, and all of a sudden, you're being attacked.

During this phase, you're no longer so incredible and no longer receiving all the adoring texts or emails, and if you question that, you are also criticized. They tell you they are busy or have work to do, yet you are supposed to respond to them immediately whenever they reach out.

The manipulation and gaslighting will begin during this stage.

Gaslighting is a tool that all narcissists use for the express purpose of manipulating their targets into believing that what they believed was reality is not, so that they begin to question their own sanity. The term comes from Patrick Hamilton's 1938 play *Gas Light*. In the play, which is set in the Victorian era, a husband attempts to make his wife believe she is losing her sanity by dimming the gas lamps in the home. She comments to the husband that the lamp was just lit moments ago, and he tells her that it was not and that she is imagining things.

Here are some sample types of phrases that narcissists will use for this purpose:

"You're not seeing things in the right way."
"That's not how that happened."
"Everyone else thinks..."
"No one else thinks..."
"You're way too needy."
"You're way too sensitive."
"You can't take a joke."
"I'm the only one you can trust."
"No one else has your back like I do."

They will infuse "loving thoughts" and "affection" during this phase as well, but just the bare minimum—just enough to keep you going. They are quite adept at reading what the bare minimum is to keep you interested and present, so that you continue to be what they need you to be for them.

Those who provide "supply" to the narcissist are treated as if they are part of the narcissist (meaning you belong to them) and are expected to live up to those expectations. Narcissists see their supply as their possession, which is why they have no boundaries when it comes to their supply.

The purpose of this phase is to continue the programming and get you more under their power and control. The grooming and conditioning are continuing here. It's highly likely that you are an empathic person. They often prey upon targets who are going to want to "save" them or "help" them, or who are kind, generous people. Then when they rage on you, have tantrums, treat you poorly, or act irresponsibly, they can blame it on having a horrible childhood, a terrible ex, bad circumstances, or whatever, and you will feel sorry for them and want to help them. That will go a long way for them. They will not only get away with their bad behavior, but you end up doing everything for them, plus you pour love and affection into them. They win all around. More on this in Chapter 3.

The "Discard" Phase

Get ready to become Public Enemy Number One. Whether you are doing the discarding or they are, the wrath, it is a-coming. Hell hath no fury like a narcissist scorned. For one thing, abandonment is what they fear most. Narcissists also see things in black and white, according to Bill Eddy in *Splitting*, meaning you are either for them or against them. If you are against them, then you are their enemy. The Discard Phase is the final stage of the narcissist's relationship and is by far the most painful for you.

During this phase, the narcissist will want to take you down before you can take them down. This is where you see the birth of the smear campaign, meaning where they go to third parties (sometimes called "flying monkeys") and start to try to get people to be on their side and against you. That narcissistic injury is really triggered here, and you can really see the narcissistic rage come flying out.

Their behavior may become quite erratic at this time also. If you are the one doing the discarding, you may see anything from last minute love bombing in an attempt to get you to change your mind to attempts to make you feel guilty. They may blow up your phone, show up at your work, stalk you, or worse, threaten you or even try to harm you. If they are the ones doing the discarding, they will move on to the next form of supply source as fast as possible, especially if the narcissist perceives that person as a "better" source of supply and one that they can flaunt to the old source of supply.

Caution! Caution! You will feel used and abused during this time. They can and will drop you faster than a hot potato sometimes here, even if you have given them the moon and all the stars in the universe. Then they will turn around and say they gave all of that to you. It will be super painful. You will not get closure. You will not get them to acknowledge anything they ever did to you. Remember the **Four Fs**:

Forget About:

1. Telling them they are a narcissist. This just opens a can of worms—and then of course they will spin the conversation around so that *you* become the narcissist.

Forget About:

2. Closure. (I personally had a hard time with this one. I thought I would be able to wrap up my relationship nicely and cordially with the narcissistic business partner, but this does not happen. They are not capable of happy endings.)

Forget About:

3. Getting them to see they are wrong or to have any regret about their behavior. (Even if they say sorry, it's all a manipulation and a "faux-pology." Don't fall for it. They are liars and can't help their narcissistic behavior. No contact is the way. Cut off the supply source and get what you want through applying the SLAY Method®, then move on with your life.)

Forget About:

4. Them seeing your side or what you contributed to the relationship. (It's so unsatisfying, but you just have to know what you gave and then give yourself to others in the future who appreciate you. Forgive yourself. Heal and move on.)

But during this phase, you have one of **three options**:

1. Attempt to **stay** in the relationship and make it work (not recommended). This applies to any kind of a relationship, business or personal.
2. Think you can just leave but **give them what they want**. This is a total trick. I know what you're thinking: *I*

will show them how generous I am and then that will somehow garner favor for me. No. No, it will not. They will take it, and your generosity will be forgotten. They will assume that they were entitled to whatever that was that you offered. It will not get you any sort of nice resolution. Then you will be stuck in this lopsided situation and *still* not be done, because more than likely they will continue to want to get supply from you. Now you're mad because of the unfair circumstances you're in. Listen, they were liars when you were in the business or personal relationship with them. They will be way worse now. Even if they say they want to resolve it "amicably." It's an insidious game designed to continue to get supply from you, and it will never end.

3. **Fight back to get a fair result**. But do it in a way that is super strategic. This way ultimately ends with cutting off all supply sources so that you can move forward with your life. This is the only way that you will be able to finally have peace. If done properly, the narcissist will be begging you to resolve the issues so that you can do this *without backlash*. This does take time and planning. There is no magic wand when it comes to negotiating the right way in *any* realm, unfortunately, but especially with narcissists.

Pretty much the entire rest of this book is going to be about what to do during the Discard Phase, so I will continue the discussion as we go along, but here's what I want to reiterate at this point: because narcissists are already in "survival mode" to begin with, and because of their deep fear of abandonment, they will do almost anything to protect themselves during the Discard Phase.

There are some other very highly important ideas that I must distinguish here also.

Hierarchy of Narcissistic Supply

As I explained earlier, narcissistic supply is anything that feeds a narcissist's ego. Because narcissists have no sense of internal value, they feel like they must extrapolate all their value from sources outside of themselves. That feeling of deficiency and emptiness inside of them is like a beast that must constantly be fed, and they use people to feed that beast.

The black hole inside of them is like a bottomless pit. They are so desperate for you to fill it, and you, as this empath who probably also experienced some sort of trauma in your life, also probably want to fill it and "save" them in some way, but this hole cannot be filled. Whatever you put in is never enough.

This is why narcissists are sometimes referred to as **Energy Vampires**. Before I had the language to even know what I was dealing with when it came to my covert, passive-aggressive business partner, I remember I kept thinking of the word "leech." I felt like she was a leech sucking the life out of me. You feel totally drained when you are in these relationships, because they are constantly manipulating the situation so that all your energy is directed one way: toward them. The river of your energy has to flow one direction and one direction only.

But there is a hierarchy to narcissistic supply—there is one type of supply the narcissist values over the other.

On the top, there is what I refer to as **Diamond Level Narcissistic Supply**. This pertains to how narcissists look to the world. Diamond Level Supply is Grade-A supply. Narcissists will protect and defend this form of supply at any cost. This is anything that enhances the outside world's perception of the narcissist. Examples of Diamond Level Supply would be:

> *The narcissist's public reputation with employers/employees*
> *Prestigious careers*
> *Impressive friends (especially celebrities)*
> *Accomplishments (even if made up, lied about, or attained by unethical means)*
> *Huge bank accounts (again, even if attained by cheating others)*
> *Winning (especially in public forums that matter)*
> *Adulation (of any kind)*
> *Having a spouse that others covet*
> *Receiving lots of public attention (i.e., being a celebrity)*

By the way, if you are litigating a case, Diamond Level Supply usually also extends to how they look to the judge in your case. They don't want to look bad to a judge or to a jury. Nor do they normally want to look bad to either lawyer (yours or their own), nor to the mediator if you have one, nor to anyone else involved in your case. Usually, their modus operandi is to try to charm everyone involved into believing that they are the "good" one and that *you* are the "crazy" one. More on that later....

The second form of supply is what I refer to as **Coal Level Narcissistic Supply**. Coal Level Narcissistic Supply in a nutshell basically refers to the energy narcissists receive by insulting, degrading, controlling, and manipulating others. This is also *very* important to narcissists. They do want it all. But if push comes to shove, they will give this form up to save the Diamond Level Supply. We will get much more into this when we come to **L: Leverage**. For now, I want to address what Coal Level Narcissistic Supply is. This is the dark underbelly of supply. This is what the narcissist saves just for their targets.

I always think of this as the **Deadly Three Ds—devaluing, debasing, and degrading**. This is part of the devalue phase, obviously, and where narcissists get off on controlling people, because they are getting fed from this. Remember this is a source of "supply" from them. Anywhere that they are getting a source of supply is a place that they will stay. They are like vultures. If there is a food source to be had there, then there they will be.

This is a food source for them in so many ways. They make the target doubt themselves. They exhaust the victim into submission by tricking them. You ultimately feel utterly and completely devoid of energy, as if a leech has sucked the blood from your body.

You must, must, must, must remember that! Examples of Coal Level Supply are:

Insults
Passive aggression
Purposely provoking chaos
Triggering emotional reactions in you
Demeaning behaviors and words
Manipulation and intimidation tactics
Using children as weapons
Refusing to provide discovery in court cases
Filing fraudulent false pleadings
Lying about you to third parties
Ghosting you in texts/emails
Stalking, yelling, criticism
Mind games
Ignoring your needs
Withholding money
Threats of violence
Hiding money
Gaslighting

The Biggest Myth about Negotiating with Narcissists

The biggest myth about negotiating with narcissists is that they just want to win. They do want to win for the *optics* (see my explanation about Diamond Level Narcissistic Supply above), but—and this a *huge but*—they also enjoy the process of watching you squirm and intimidating you.

They will not give up their Coal Level Supply without a fight.

This is precisely why the regular way of negotiating *fails*. You cannot simply apply the rules of negotiating with non-narcissistic people, such as listening with empathy and providing value, and think that will work without more of a strategy and a real plan of action. Listen here: *it won't.*

Narcissists want to take you down. They want to manipulate you, intimidate you, and continue to get Coal Level Supply from you. Even if it means taking themselves down in the process! They do not think like rational people!

We will be circling back to this, but I wanted to be sure to clarify this now: *narcissists adeptly use people and any means possible and necessary to wring every piece of narcissistic supply that they can out of every situation, regardless of the cost to others or themselves.*

Unfortunately, for those of us dealing with narcissists, we go into a relationship naively thinking we are dealing with a reasonably prudent person (stop thinking that!), realizing way too late that we are not, trying to scramble to catch up (and meanwhile they are already way ahead of the game), then realizing that a lot of their tactics are often hard to prove.

It's absolutely maddening, because there often is this element of plausible deniability, leaving their victims thinking, *Why even bother? I can never win!*

Okay, so here's the thing. I know how you're feeling.

Would you like me to articulate it even further for you? Just so that you know that I really do know. I hear from people every day, so here is a sampling of how people feel when they start.

It has been an emotional rollercoaster.
I have been walking on eggshells.
It has been a very dark place.
I feel used and abused.
I feel stupid, small, and overwhelmed.
I want to end my life.
Everyone just believes their lies.
I feel torn, and completely unsure of everything.
I feel like there's something innately wrong with me.
I feel hopeless and helpless and totally unworthy.
They make me feel like everything is all my fault.
I feel totally oppressed and like it's all my fault.
I'm completely exhausted.
They lie to the point that it's shocking, yet everyone believes them.
I feel like I'm losing and just want to give up.
I feel like I'm going crazy and like I'm unlovable.
It has now affected me physically and caused me to have autoimmune issues.
I feel full of shame and inadequacy.
Out of control.
A devastation I never knew was possible.
Totally alone, because no one else understands what I am going through.

How did I do? Have I got it right? See, I got you. I told you I know how you feel.

Let me say right out of the gate: none of the above are true. It's not your fault. Yes, we can turn this around. Yes, there is hope.

Listen, regardless of whether you are trying to negotiate with a narcissist in a divorce, for a business contract, with a neighbor, a boss, a colleague, a family member, or whomever, it is never easy. In fact, it is pure hell.

That's the bad news.

Here's the good news.

Applying the right strategy will have you SLAYing the narcissistic bully every time.

By becoming aware of the signs and symptoms of their behavior, we can create a plan, apply a framework, box them in by building an invisible fence around them when they aren't even aware of it, then spring our leverage on them. Then pounce! We got them!

By the end of this book, you will look at every single one of those statements I wrote above and go, *Wow, that was the old me. I don't even recognize that person anymore.*

Here's probably how you *want* to feel, based on some of things that I hear the most from clients:

I want to feel whole.
I want to feel healthy.
I want to feel powerful.
I'm ready to feel acknowledged.
I just want to be able to breathe.
I just want relief.
It would be nice to feel cherished.
I want to feel complete.
I want to feel valued.
I am ready to feel empowered and inspired.
I want to be respected.

I just want what's fair.
I want to feel safe.
I want to feel light and in flow.
I want to feel joy.
I want peace.
I want to feel creative.
I want meaning in my life.
I just want to be loved for who I am.
I want to be in a beautiful loving and giving relationship.

You can absolutely get there. You *will* absolutely get there.

I will be holding your hand every single step of the way, guiding you.

But here's the thing: SLAYing negotiations with narcissists is a simple process, but not an easy process. It's tedious and meticulous. It's so hard, because, depending on how long you've been in a relationship with a narcissist, they may have totally done a number on you. You may be dealing with serious trauma or, as one of my coaching clients called it, "scrambled eggs for brains." That's why, next up in Chapter 3, I am going to go through, in very specific detail, many of the methodologies that narcissists engage in to destabilize you, then gain control over you.

Awareness is the first line of attack to shifting the paradigm.

What Can You Do Now to Start SLAYing?

1. Start keeping track of every single email and text from or about your narcissist. Keep copies of everything.
2. Put passwords on everything, including your computers, telephones, cloud devices, emails, and social media—and change the passwords often.

3. Start doing some self-care to feel better, such as taking naps when you need them and giving yourself permission to engage in personal growth exercises or other tools for self-reflection, such as meditation or yoga.
4. Make sure you have a good support system in place personally and/or professionally (such as a therapist or clergy).
5. Set aside some time to journal for a few minutes each day.
6. Reflect on how you want to feel—write down one or two of your top feelings. Stay focused on those feelings. Look at those feelings every single day.

Mantra for Today:

I am a powerful expression of what's possible.
(Or write one of your own that speaks to you....)

CHAPTER 3

FLYING MONKEYS, GASLIGHTING, WORD SALAD, AND MORE (A.K.A. METHODS NARCISSISTS USE TO DESTABILIZE YOU AND TAKE CONTROL)

"The narcissist devours people, consumes their output, and casts the empty, writhing shells aside."
SAM VAKNIN

In order to introduce this chapter, and at this point in this book, I want to make a few bold statements in some very, very simplistic ways that I haven't up until this point.

Number One: One of the absolute biggest problems with negotiating with narcissists is surprisingly *not* the narcissists. It's the people around the narcissists who continue to try to interact with them as if they are not narcissists and expect them to act like and feel like they themselves do. That's like saying just because snakes and eels look alike, they are the same. They are not.

We need to educate not just laypersons who are interacting with narcissists (and who are drowning while trying sometimes), but also attorneys, judges, mediators, managers at all organizational levels, C-level executives, medical professionals, teachers, and clergy. Frankly, there are quite a few mental health professionals that I have come across who have shared with me that they have a very scant education in narcissism. I also believe that teens should be taught about this in schools.

Why do I say this? Because narcissists are narcissists. They will not change. Thus, the rest of *us* must change how we respond, manage, and interact with them.

Number Two: For the people who do have to negotiate with narcissists, it is absolutely imperative to understand that the playing field is not level. Narcissists fight dirty. If this were a physical fight, and you were two kids wrestling on the ground, they would be the ones biting, pulling hair, and kicking you in the groin. Thus, coming at them *directly* is *not* the smart strategy. That is the *naive* strategy.

Number Three: For the professionals who are involved in litigation, such as judges, mediators, arbitrators, and attorneys, it is crucial to appreciate the difference between parties who are mentally healthy (and therefore, at least have a much higher chance of wanting an actual resolution from negotiations—much more on this in Chapter 6 on Leverage) and negotiations where one or both of the parties suffers from some level of narcissistic personality disorder.

Number Four: Finally, for those of you who have battled narcissists, the way they take over your brains and bodies is stealthy, insidious, and masterful. You really are almost powerless to their level of skill. They have studied you and know exactly how to present themselves.

Using something called Narcissistic Mirroring, during the love bombing stage, like a chameleon, they shape and conform themselves to look and sound like you, so you like them more. They use facial expressions like yours and body language like yours, because they want you to feel so connected to them. (This is why you *must* forgive yourself for falling for them—yes, they are *that* good.)

As I said in Chapter 2, once you enter into the Discard Phase, they become even worse. That narcissistic injury becomes triggered, the narcissistic rage comes flying out, then you become Public Enemy Number One. That's when you're in the war, and you are the target of a full-on assault. Get ready for a massive, grievous, aggressive, and offensive attack on you,

Here's the problem. If you've already been in a relationship with a narcissist, very likely it has already affected you in every possible way—physically, emotionally, and even spiritually. You're already utterly and entirely depleted.

But it's even more than simple exhaustion.

While I mentioned in Chapter 2 that negotiating with narcissists is totally different from negotiating with non-narcissistic people because of their hidden agendas to continue to extract as much supply from you as possible in the form of Coal Level Supply, there is also another reason that negotiating with narcissists is completely distinguishable from any other kind of negotiation: they have very often spent months or even years conditioning, weakening, and destabilizing their targets so as to create an unfair advantage in the negotiations.

This is so important when it comes time to negotiate with narcissists, because you must understand how they are thinking in order to begin to build Strategy, create Leverage, Anticipate what they will do, be two steps ahead of them, and focus on You and your position.

Narcissists use a variety of methods that can even lead to long term psychological trauma or c-PTSD (Complex Post-Traumatic Stress Disorder). The difference between PTSD and c-PTSD is that PTSD is a condition that occurs in a person after a single event. To clarify, for example, PTSD is something one might experience after an accident or after having been sexually assaulted. C-PTSD, on the other hand, is something one experiences after having been repeatedly traumatized over a long period of time.

People who have c-PTSD can experience difficulty with sleep, flashbacks, problems with emotional regulation, impairment in alertness and reactivity, a re-experiencing of the trauma, difficulty in performing regular daily tasks sometimes, migraines, and feeling hopeless, and it can even impact mental acuity.

Even if you don't have c-PTSD, you can experience symptoms of what is known as **cognitive dissonance** as a result of the narcissist's *manipulation tools*, most of which will be explained in this chapter. (The *tools* are used by almost all narcissists in such a strikingly similar way that I sometimes caustically refer to them not only as the narcissist's tools, but actually as their "to do" list.)

Cognitive dissonance is a phenomenon that is a common occurrence for people who have been subjected to abuse by narcissists long term, where they no longer trust their own perception of reality as the truth, because it has been distorted by the narcissist for so long. Put another way, they don't trust that what they are perceiving with their own senses is correct anymore, which causes them to feel confusion. It's utterly traumatic.

Thus, when it comes time to negotiate with the toxic person, it is clearly not the same as two reasonable, mentally healthy people coming to the table. Because very few people understand narcissism, and even fewer understand the *impact* that narcissists have on the people around them, the majority of the people who are negotiating expect everyone to be negotiating as though everyone involved is a mentally strong, healthy person!

Okay, so with that foundation laid, this is why I wanted to dedicate an entire chapter to just some of the methods that narcissists employ, or dare I say, deploy, upon their prey, in order to take control. It really is a subtle taking over—almost like cult leaders do with their victims.

One other note: while many people refer to the people who end up in relationships with narcissists as "victims," you may have noticed that I tend not to like that particular word. While it may just be semantics, I prefer to use the word target. Here's why.

Narcissists are predators. They chose a form of supply that had a lot of value. You are not a victim forever. You are a person who will not only survive this temporary situation, but you will overcome it and be so much stronger as a result.

Narcissists, by and large, are not people who can be rehabilitated. They will have to live with themselves. You, on the other hand, will take your pain and turn it into a purpose that you have yet to see. I have worked with clients who have been terrorized by narcissists and who are now living proof that narcissists don't get the last word.

My client, Peter, for example, was dealing with two malignant narcissists. One of the narcissists was his wife, and one of them was *his mother, who had teamed up with his wife against him.* It started off where I actually thought my client was the one who needed to behave. He came in because his wife had filed a restraining order against him. She had cheated on him. He found out and then slashed her tires while she was staying at the boyfriend's house. A very bad fact. Divorce cases often start off this way. A huge bang. Not odd. But oddly, his wife was staying with *his mother.* Very strange, but okay.

Then it turns out that his wife's attorney's fees are being paid by *his mother.* Even more weird. The next thing you know, the night before the hearing on whether this temporary restraining order against him is going to become permanent, she comes over to the marital home at 11 p.m., where he's staying, and lets herself in with her key, on the pretense that she needs "medicine" for their son, who is staying with her at *his mother's house.*

Startled, my client pulled out his cell phone and started videotaping. He knew she wasn't supposed to be near him and asked her on tape what she was doing there. You could see her on the video then go into the kitchen and pick up a knife. He then followed her into the master bedroom where she went into the closet, took his clothes, and started throwing them on the floor. He just watched her and filmed. She then turned to him and started attacking him. In the video, you could hear him yell, "I'm being attacked!" and then her yell back, "Yup! You're being attacked!" Then the camera shut off.

Directly after that, the police were called, and *she was arrested.* The restraining order that she had tried to file against him? Obviously dropped.

That same day, the wife went out and filed for another one! This time, she actually prevailed and got it! Even though he had the videotape. He, of course, then filed for divorce and asked for custody.

In the meantime, his own mother left an ominous voicemail on his phone, threatening that if he didn't drop the divorce and the custody claim, she would make sure that this woman that they knew he had been in a relationship with would be "deported." Apparently, she was from the Czech Republic and had been in the country based upon a marriage to another guy, and my client's mother and wife were going to somehow try to report to immigration that it had been a sham marriage.

This case became such a maze of twists and turns, filled with such shock and awe, that we spent the next several years with our jaws on the ground nearly daily. This entire book could be on just this case. Our client ended up wrongfully jailed, not once, but twice. It involved crooked cops and crooked prosecutors. The levels of despicability ran deep here. We even discovered that the mother paid a private investigator to sleep with the wife so that the PI would say that the husband had been near the marital home in violation of the restraining order. The PI's affidavit caused the husband to be arrested and wrongfully jailed. We didn't realize that the PI was sleeping with the wife until much later.

Peter's mother's incentive? To get custody of his children. Apparently, her husband, a prominent surgeon, had had an affair with a nurse, and somehow, in her warped mind, she thought that wrestling custody of her grandchildren away from her son and daughter-in-law would "save her marriage." Additionally, she was supporting all her adult children, as a way of manipulating them, and my client was the only one who had become quite successful on his own and no longer needed her money. Thus, he no longer wanted to be under her control either. Oh, and she also was a malignant narcissist, who just happened to get off by watching people squirm and suffer while she ruined their lives.

The wife's incentive? Pure survival. She had no means of supporting herself. The wife was also a total narcissist who was in collusion with the mother-in-law. Mother-in-law was paying the bills, and she figured if MIL was going to pay all the fees, then she'd end up with custody and live with them. She had apparently gone to live with them when she was sixteen years old, so relying on Peter's parents was nothing new for her, and that was the plan they had hatched.

There were many times—let me tell you, many times—that Peter wanted to give up. He felt total despair.

He felt like the entire world was against him.

He truly had almost no one. He had one cousin and his girlfriend. Plus, our team.

Day in and day out, the assaults came.

How long did the case last? Four years.

How much did it cost him in fees? Hundreds of thousands. Not just for me, but for criminal attorneys, forensic accountants for his businesses, private investigators, and more.

He went months without seeing his children sometimes.

His emotions ran the gamut. Sadness. Anger. Depression. Abject fear. Resentment. Rage.

He was constantly asking me what I thought was going to happen. He was constantly ruminating about what the *what ifs*.

But here's what I said to him at one point during his case, and I'm saying this to you now too.

No one, and I mean no one, can help you win if you don't believe you can win.

They only win if you give in.

Once you start to identify what a narcissist is and what it is you're dealing with, the corner starts to turn. Quickly.

I don't like the term *victim*, because I know the power of words.

What follows the words "I am" is everything.

You are not a victim.

You were a target.

You are a survivor.

You are a winner.

Start saying, "I am victorious."

In the end, Peter got custody and ultimate decision-making over education for the children.

The Final Judgment stated, "The court finds the Husband's testimony credible, and that his mother has interfered and/or acted to thwart or disrupt the Husband's relationship with the parties' minor children," and that the wife had worked "diligently to thwart the father/sons' relationship."

Keep believing it can happen. Because it can. It did for Peter. It can and will for you too.

Now, here are just some of the methods narcissists use to destabilize you to take control.

True Self Versus False Self

To understand why narcissists need to control you, it's important to understand the concept of the true self versus the false self. Sam Vaknin, author of *Malignant Self Love: Narcissism Revisited*, says that he is a narcissist himself and explains that the false self is the person that narcissists create early on in their lives, in order for them to feel like they can survive. It's the person they "want" to be.

The "true self," then, is their inner self, the shamed one, the one they desperately are hiding all the time, and the one whom they hate. The false self is the one they display to the world, the one who must gain control over people, and the one who demands adulation. The true self, to the narcissist, is one who is weak, shriveled, useless, and disgusting. This true self must be hidden away at all costs and is never to be revealed.

Vaknin further explains that that false self is the proxy—the decoy, if you will—who attracts people. It is the "invention" of the child to protect themselves from the trauma that is being inflicted upon them at the time.

As Dr. Malkin pointed out, narcissism is on a continuum, and in the case of true narcissists, the true self has been smothered and stamped down, in order to survive. In truly whole and healthy people, the true self is the only self. This is the genuine one, where you know who you are as a soul, where you feel and know from your core that you are inherently valuable. There is no false self that exists.

On the other end of the spectrum is a narcissist, where almost no true self exists, because the false self has nearly killed the true self. When asked why narcissists aren't prone to suicide, Vaknin explained that the "simple answer is that they died a long time ago…" and that "[n]arcissists are the true zombies of the world."

Trauma Bonding

One of the other ways that narcissists destabilize you is through trauma bonding. This is another reason why negotiating with narcissists is completely different from negotiating with mentally healthy people. Trauma bonding occurs between an abuser and a victim. It is an emotional attachment, a connection, that an abused person has to their abuser, as a result of intermittent, recurring, cyclical reinforcement. It can be in romantic or platonic relationships. This is where the abuser provides affection, love, or validation but then intersperses it with punishment and abuse repeatedly.

As I explained in Chapter 2, narcissists have a pattern of relationships that begin with the Love bomb Phase, which quickly moves into the Devalue Phase and ends with the Discard Phase. But the relationship is not linear. It's not love bombing, then devaluing, then discarding. The relationship always begins with love bombing and always ends with the discard, which can be done by either party. But in between, the narcissist moves back and forth between all the phases.

More specifically, the narcissist will love bomb, then devalue, then go back to love bombing when necessary, then devalue, then go into discarding at times, but then love bomb if necessary, and so on and so on. Thus, the relationship might look like this:

Love Bomb
Devalue
Love Bomb
Devalue
Love Bomb
Discard
Love Bomb
Devalue
Love Bomb
Discard

It really all depends on what is required of them in the moment to get what they want.

The experience for the target is a horrific rollercoaster of emotions. You experience the most incredible highs of your life followed by the most unbelievable cruelty. Back and forth. Back and forth. With no explanation, provocation, understanding, or predictability, this becomes your life. You will spend your life trying hard to measure up, to be better next time, to up the ante, to fill that black hole, thinking it's your fault. Until you've had enough and decide you're walking away, and they beg and plead and say they will be better, and you believe them, but they are far worse the next time. Back and forth. Back and forth. Eggshells.

Robert Sapolsky, a psychologist from Stanford University, did a study on monkeys. In one test group the monkeys were rewarded and received a treat each and every time they did something good. In measuring the dopamine levels, the feel-good hormone, in their brains, there was no change. In the other test group, the monkeys were rewarded and received a treat when they did something good—but this time just intermittently. They didn't know when they were going to receive a reward. In this study, what he found was that it wasn't receiving the treat itself, but rather the *anticipation* that they were going to receive the treat, that caused the dopamine levels in their brains to rise to the level of that of being on *cocaine*. In other words, it wasn't receiving the treat itself, but rather the anticipation—or actually, the *anxiety*.

Thus, the narcissist's intermittent "nice" behavior, or love bombing, causes the anticipation of receiving that hit of reward in our brains that will cause the dopamine to be released at the same levels as cocaine does. In other words, we can become physiologically *addicted* to the other person. This is another reason why oftentimes negotiating with a narcissist or communicating with a narcissist is inherently different from negotiating with others.

If you are dealing with the effects of a trauma bond, then it is essential to recognize this and extricate yourself from the situation so that you are prepared to negotiate and communicate on a more level playing field prior to entering into the ring with this other person.

Gaslighting

As I stated in Chapter 2, gaslighting is a manipulation tool used by all narcissists.

Gaslighting can take on many different forms, but it is always designed to do the same thing: distort reality, invalidate, and confuse a target. If it happens to you over a long enough period of time, your brain can become foggy, and you can even start to question your sanity.

This is such a huge part of the narcissist's tool bag that I could spend an entire chapter, and even perhaps a book, on just gaslighting alone. It shows up in a variety of ways. But basically, the intent is to make you feel like you're crazy.

Twisting Details

One form of gaslighting is to twist details about the way that things took place. In this form, the narcissist is either deconstructing or reconstructing events to the point that you begin to question your memory and eventually your sanity. It's a totally alternate version of reality to suit the narrative they want to paint. Here are some examples.

1. *You find out that your husband has made plans to go out of town with the guys for your anniversary weekend. When you question him about it, he says that you discussed it and you agreed to it. You know that you never had such a conversation. You know this never happened, but they keep insisting, and you begin to feel as if you can't trust your memory.*
2. *You find out that your business partner went behind your back and started working with certain vendors that you specifically agreed neither of you would work with. When you question your partner about it, your partner says you discussed waiting until the end of the year, but that now would be an optimum time to get going with them, and they knew you would be on board. You know that conversation never happened in that way at all.*

Invalidating Statements

Gaslighting can also take the form of invalidating statements. These statements discount your version of reality or your feelings about a certain topic. The narcissist is often trying to make you feel as if you have no right to feel the way that you do. In this form of gaslighting, there is a bit of plausible deniability (meaning there is no clear evidence to prove that they were ever involved in any way). They act wide-eyed and innocent, and if anybody questions them, they respond with, "What? I didn't say anything." Here are some examples of this form of gaslighting:

> *"You're too sensitive."*
> *"Can't you take a joke?"*
> *"I never did (or said) that. You're imagining things."*
> *"We discussed that, and you agreed. (Or you said ________)"*
> *"You're way too emotional."*
> *"Your tone is off."*
> *"You're shouting."*
> *"You're just insecure."*
> *"You're just jealous."*
> *"You're making too much of things."*
> *"You're just crazy."*
> *"You're PMSing." (Or "Are you on your period?")*
> *"You're just crazy."*
> *"It's your fault because [you don't give me enough sex, your attitude is rotten, you're always mad, etcetera....]"*
> *"That never happened."*
> *"You're delusional."*
> *"You're a narcissist."*
> *"You don't know the facts."*
> *"You don't know the full story."*

"Your [trusted source] is lying. I'm telling you the truth."
"Everyone else thinks ________________________"
"No one else thinks _________________________"

Projection and Deflection

Projection and deflection are other forms of gaslighting. This is where you try to bring up a topic for which they should be responsible, and then blame shifts to someone else. It's *always* someone else's fault, and many times they find it to be *your* fault. Whatever you accuse them of, that's what *you* are now doing, or that's what *you are.*

Another way they will deflect is to constantly shift the conversation so that you can never get to the topic you want to discuss. This kind of deflection reminds me of the line from the song "How Do You Solve a Problem Like Maria?" in *The Sound of Music*, where they answer the titular question with "How do you catch a wave and pin it down?" In other words, you can't.

Here's a sample conversation to highlight what deflecting and projecting are:

You: *I need to talk to you about these suspicious text messages.*
Narcissist: *Why are you bringing that up now?*
You: *When else would be a good time?*
Narcissist: *You literally just interrupted.*
You: *I didn't interrupt you.*
Narcissist: *That was so rude.*
You: *Can we talk about the texts?*
Narcissist: *Now you're raising your voice.*
You: *I didn't raise my voice.*

Narcissist: *Oh my gosh. Now you're so emotional. I can't deal with you when you're so emotional.*

Word Salad

Narcissistic Word Salad is sometimes referred to as a verbal assassination. One form of word salad is circular conversation that goes nowhere, which looks like constant belaboring of a point that you thought was settled and proven over and over, and then over and over again. For example, the narcissist questions why you were late, and you tell them it was because you were visiting your sister in the hospital. You tell them all about the conversation and show them texts to prove it all, so you think the conversation is settled.

Then, a half an hour later, the narcissist will again bring up that you were purposely late, just to trigger you and try to get you to be drawn into an emotional and psychological battle. Here you thought the issue was settled, but the narcissist will bring it up again and again and again to try to make you feel guilty and to sadistically manipulate you. If you say you proved that you had an "alibi," they may say that you didn't, or go into some other ways that you're horrible for disrespecting them and not showing up when you're supposed to, how many other times it has happened, and on and on.

Another technique that narcissists use for word salad is just a complete lack of logic. In this one, they will bring something up that has no basis in fact whatsoever, and you find yourself defending yourself. Many times, they will accuse you of things they themselves are doing. For example, a fan favorite with narcissists is to accuse you of cheating. You find yourself defending yourself, saying, "What the heck are you talking about? I was at lunch with my mother and my sister, and you know that. You know that I was. I was texting you the whole time. I sent you pictures of myself from there."

Even if you did send photos from lunch, they may accuse you of these types of things, and you find that you have to defend yourself against such completely baseless claims that came out of thin air. In other words, their claims have absolutely no logic whatsoever. Then you find yourself defending yourself, and suddenly you're in this utter verbal chaos as if you're in Twilight Zone.

Ghosting

Ghosting is a sadistic maneuver that starts early on in a narcissistic relationship. This happens right after the love bombing ends. During the love bombing stage, the narcissist literally cannot be in communication with you enough. They flood your inbox and your phone with text messages to the point where you are almost overwhelmed with how often you hear from them. If you don't respond right away, they wonder why. During this initial phase, even if the narcissistic relationship is a business relationship, you are so filled with excitement because you are constantly hearing from them. Every day, you receive ideas from them. They are so over the moon and crazy with excitement, and so are you!

Then once they have locked you into position somehow and they know they have you, the waves come crashing down.

Suddenly. Poof. Like magic. They're gone!

Where'd they go?

You text them, and they don't text back.

You email them, and...nothing. No response.

They are totally gone, and you are wondering what happened. When you finally do hear back from them, they are annoyed.

They make you feel needy. Suddenly, the dynamics have shifted.

This is part of the hot/cold game that narcissists play. Round and round and up and down this game will go, all the way till the bitter end.

The Smear Campaign and Flying Monkeys

During the discard phase of the narcissist's relationship is when you see the birth of the Smear Campaign. The smear campaign is when the narcissist will smear the target publicly in an effort to attempt to persuade people to believe that the target is a heinous and horrible person, that the falling out was all the target's fault, that the narcissist was wronged by the target, that the target is evil, that the narcissist should be canonized as a saint and did everything right in the relationship, and, well, you get the idea.

The "Flying Monkeys" is a term that comes from the weird, winged creatures that hung around the Wicked Witch of the West in *The Wizard of Oz*. They were part of her squad. These were her messengers, who would report back to her on what people in the kingdom were doing. In the world of narcissism, flying monkeys are similar, to a certain extent. These are people being used by narcissists against the target person to make them feel ganged up on and isolated.

So, to be clear, they are using other people to make their targets or victims feel like they are going crazy and to try to destabilize them, control them, abuse them, and hurt them in this particular choice of emotional abuse warfare.

The use of the flying monkeys serves many purposes:

They bolster the appearance that "everyone else" believes the narcissist and everything that comes out of their mouth.

They bolster the appearance that "no one else" believes anything that you have to say, nor will they. They will believe the lies of the narcissist.

You feel bullied and ganged up on.

You feel more and more isolated.

You feel more and more crazy.

You feel like it's pointless to advance any position that's different from the narcissist's, because you won't ever be able to beat them, because they have this army of people who are on their side.

The narcissist uses flying monkeys continuously, as needed, throughout the relationship. However, during the "discard" phase of the relationship, the narcissists heighten their efforts, often dramatically increasing their usage of flying monkeys. But here's the sneaky thing: the smear campaign often begins long before the target realizes it has begun. This is because the narcissist will anticipate that the discard is going to happen and will start "planting seeds," sometimes several months ahead of time. All narcissists use flying monkeys, but covert narcissists are probably the most adept at how they use them, often painting their smear as "concern."

Here's an example of how they might start planting a seed long before the actual discard:

> *"I am so concerned about how much Fred had to drink last night. I'm just so worried about him because I care about him so much."*

Then six months later…

> *"Fred is an alcoholic. I told you I was concerned about his drinking months ago. He definitely shouldn't be alone with the children. Would you mind testifying as a witness for me against him in court? We want to keep the children safe, don't we?"*

See how adept the narcissist was at planting that seed several months before? Then the narcissist just probably kept dropping pearls throughout the weeks leading up to the discard to make themselves look like the victim. Covert narcissists are masters at this. All the while, Fred would have had no idea what was going on and probably had no issues with alcohol at all.

The good news is that courts still want to see actual *proof* that someone might have an issue with alcohol, and that children would be unsafe in their care. Plus, what people tell others is considered hearsay, and on and on. None of that would likely hold up in court on a "best interests of a child" claim, but it is frightening that they start these campaigns so long beforehand, and the targets have no idea what's happening.

The bad news about the above scenario is that Fred will end up spending a whole lot of time having to deal with defending against the claims that he's an alcoholic. Really, the worst part is the mental and emotional warfare, the feeling like the narcissist has these minions who are believing everything that they say, who are reporting back to them, and who are lined up on their side.

Honestly, one of the things I came to realize in the past couple of years is that oftentimes the flying monkeys have been love bombed by the narcissist just like you were. Sometimes, they have no idea what's going on, and they don't see the truth of who they are. It's almost like when Jesus was hanging on the cross and said, "Father, forgive them for they know not what they do." I think sometimes they simply don't know. Sometimes they do, but sometimes they don't.

The best thing you can do for yourself, if possible, is to just cut off contact with the flying monkeys, just the same as you are cutting off contact with the narcissist. This way, you don't have to see what's happening with the narcissist. I would block them on social media also, so that you can start to heal. The more you can block the toxicity and negativity from your life, the faster you will start to heal and move forward.

When I was dealing with a covert narcissistic business partner, I found that she was using flying monkeys quite a bit. I found myself feeling a lot of the same feelings I felt as a child when I was being bullied on the playground, quite frankly, until I realized what was going on. I truly had to distance myself from everyone whom the narcissist had a relationship with, in order to heal and move forward. I didn't even know I was dealing with a narcissist at the time. I figured that out afterward. This was something I knew I had to do instinctively, and it was the best decision I ever made. I urge you to do the same.

PSA: be very careful about what you post on social media. Flying monkeys are always lurking about and often ready to pounce and report back to the narcissist.

Remember: dealing with narcissists is like getting arrested; assume that anything you say can and will eventually be used against you.

Future Faking

Future Faking is something that narcissists usually use when they have been caught doing something wrong. They will promise to be better in the "future." It is an empty promise that they give to just get out of taking responsibility for something in the moment—a promise that they have no intention of keeping but that satisfies their target for the moment and keeps them happy for a time. They might keep some of the promises for a time. For example, the promise might be that they will go to marriage counseling for anger management. Then they do it for a period and drop out as soon as they can.

If you are in business with them, they will promise to step up their game, start making the sales they are supposed to be making, or bring the fire to the business you've always wanted them to. Whatever they know you want to hear, it will be said, and in the way they know you want to hear it.

This manipulation strategy can also be used during the love bombing or idealization phase. If you are in business with the person, the narcissist may detail a vision for how things will be if you partner with them, or the kinds of contacts that they will bring to you. If it is a romantic relationship, you may sit in a French restaurant and plan out your entire future together. How romantic and wonderful it will all be!

Future faking is a lure, a fraud in the inducement. A bait and switch.

An empty promise that goes nowhere.

The "Faux-pology"

Do narcissists say sorry? And if they do, do they really mean it? The answer to the first question is yes. The answer to the second question is…not so much. Narcissists do apologize from time to time, but they have learned to use apologies as a form of manipulation. Many narcissists don't want to apologize at all, quite frankly, even if it would be for their own benefit. They have such a fragile sense of self, and their survival instinct is so strong, that giving that little away can often feel impossible for them—unless of course they are using the apology as part of an overall manipulation scheme.

One of the best "faux-pology" stories ever involved my narcissistic client Randy. To give you an idea of how our relationship started, after having spent more than an hour listening to him pontificating about how great he was at making money, he said, "Any wiggle room in your retainer amount?" My response? "No. But I'd be happy to give you some names of cheaper attorneys if you'd like." He decided to stay, and we moved on.

Randy and his wife Lidia had been married eighteen years, which, by Florida law, was considered to be "long-term," meaning that Lidia would be eligible for permanent alimony. Anything over seventeen years is considered long-term, and the prize or penalty (depending upon which side of the fence you are on) is permanent alimony (which means it lasts until one of the parties dies or the party cashing those monthly alimony checks remarries). It's either a life sentence (if you're the payor) or a grand prize (if you're the payee), and obviously a very hotly contested issue in nearly all cases where alimony is a possibility. Of course, other factors are considered as well. In Randy's case, however, he was definitely looking down what he considered to be both barrels of the alimony life sentence gun.

On the day of mediation, Lidia was sitting in another conference room, and we had been there over twelve hours, but we had finally reached an agreement verbally. The mediator, Chris, was also a lawyer, but had dedicated his career to mediating. He had worked hard throughout the day to get us to a place where we actually had worked through the majority of the issues. By the time he burst through the doors and asked to speak to me privately, we were just expecting a draft of the marital settlement agreement to review.

With a definite look of confusion on his face, Chris asked me to step outside the conference room to speak to him. As I walked out of the room, I looked back at my client, who had an equally puzzled expression, and told him I would be right back. Out in the now dark reception area (the receptionist had left hours before), Chris said, "I have a highly unusual offer from the wife." I steeled myself, because those words, at that time of the day, usually meant the mediation had failed. The next stop after a failed mediation in divorce? A full-blown trial. Mediation either ends in a signed agreement or an impasse, and if you reach an impasse, that means you go to trial. My mind raced. Now I was going to have to set the case for trial. did I have time to handle another trial, and would the client even want to pay the fees and costs for a major trial? But he would have no choice. Back to reality.

"What kind of unusual offer?" I asked cautiously.

"In my thirty years of practicing law, and twenty years of mediating divorce cases, I haven't ever seen this before," he started.

"Okay. What is it?" I asked again, my curiosity now thoroughly piqued and starting to blur into annoyance.

"She is willing to waive permanent alimony completely if..." and he looked at me and laughed just slightly.

"Yes?" I said, now actually annoyed.

"He apologizes to her for everything he did that caused the marriage to fail," Chris finally spit out.

Now I was truly shocked. By that point, I had handled many, many divorces. I had certainly heard my share of people who wanted people to feel remorse, to do penance, to suffer, to pay, and on and on. But an apology in exchange for a *waiver of permanent alimony*?

Unheard of.

To put it into perspective, he was going to be paying her $15,000 per month in alimony or $180,000 per year. Both parties were fifty-three years old. In Florida, the payor party can apply for a modification of permanent alimony after the age of sixty-five. Assuming Randy retired at the age of sixty-five, he still would have paid her $180,000 for twelve years.

The total over those twelve years? More than $2 million!

I went back into our tiny conference room where my client waited anxiously. I proceeded to share the unusual offer with him, thinking, obviously erroneously, that he would jump at that chance.

Nope. Wrong.

"Why would I do that?" he exclaimed upon hearing the offer.

"Because it would save you millions of dollars in permanent alimony," I replied, stating the obvious.

"I'm not doing that," he said resolutely, crossing his arms and staring at my disbelieving eyes.

I blinked, and then I took a deep breath and said calmly and deliberately, "If she just wants you to go over there, sit in the room with her alone for five minutes, give her a heartfelt apology, and in exchange, you're off the hook for permanent alimony, then that's what you're going to do. Millions of monied spouses around the country would kill to be in this position right now. So, swallow your pride, get up, walk over there, and apologize!"

With the reluctance of a teenager being forced to do chores, he slowly arose with his head down, proverbial tail between his legs, then shuffled out of the room with the mediator.

Randy would rather have paid more money in alimony than apologize.

Why? Because then he could tell the world that he was paying alimony. He's the big man! Plus, he would have still supported her that way and still had control—and he wouldn't have had to admit he was wrong about anything.

It nearly shattered his sense of self to do it.

What he ended up giving her was certainly a faux-pology. But she didn't even care. She knew it too. She squeezed it out of him.

She got what she wanted.

Most narcissists don't apologize, because they have this perception that it takes away from their little, tiny sense of self. They have an extremely tough time with it, because somehow it means that they're being exposed as not being perfect, and they just cannot bring themselves to do that.

However, you will see narcissists apologize from time to time, when they are using apologies as a means of manipulation. For example, they may apologize while future faking. "I'm sorry, and it'll never happen again! From now on, you're going to see a whole new version of me." They may use apologies during the love bombing phase, during the idealization phase, but only as a means to recover a supply source that they are desperately trying to protect or defend.

Another form of faux-apology is not an apology at all, but rather a dig at you. This is where you wanted an apology, but you don't get one that feels satisfying emotionally at all. Here are examples of that:

"I'm sorry that you feel that way."
"I'm sorry that you took it that way."
"I understand that you wanted an apology, so I'm sorry."

A "guilt-pology" is another form of faux-pology you'll see from a narcissist. This is the one that is supposed to make you feel guilty for bringing anything up about them at all. Again, highly manipulative. Here are examples of this:

"I'm sorry. I guess I'm just a horrible person."
"Everything about me is awful."
"Excuse me for trying to be a wonderful mother to you."

The truth of the matter is that narcissists will make these promises not to do things again, and then break their promises over and over. You will see that they weren't truly "sorry" almost right away. This is why I call these their apologies faux-pologies. People who are truly remorseful don't continue to behave in ways that are hurtful to you over and over, regardless of your feelings.

Hoovering

Just when you thought you had escaped, *schooop*, like a Hoover vacuum sucks pennies up, there's the narcissist, sucking you back in.

That's the "hoover" in a nutshell.

After love bombing, devaluing, and discarding, you're over in your world, minding your own "beeswax," as my dad used to say, trying to heal, like Humpty-Dumpty trying to put his pieces back together again. And months later, you get a text: "Hey, just heard our favorite song and thought of you." Or you'll get a random message like "I got my cancer test results...." followed by "Oh sorry...didn't mean to send that to you." The narcissist knows full well that you'll be baited into saying, "Oh no! What's going on?"

Sometimes the hoover isn't even direct. It may be through a third party, when you find out that the narcissist is still in touch with people that you know and asking about you or telling people things about you. This can continue even years later.

The hoover isn't always positive either. Months later, you could receive a letter stating that you ruined their life, or a lawsuit could be filed against you. They will do anything to pull you back into their world.

It is a means of grabbing that source of narcissistic supply and pulling it back in. They want to see what the waters are like for re-trapping you into their toxic webs of chaos.

They may say "I've changed" or "I'm different now." Do not fall for that!

If you've already managed to break free, keep that door shut tight and locked.

The Takeaway

Here's the takeaway from this chapter put in the simplest words possible.

Announcement to the World:

We cannot continue to have one set of rules for negotiation that applies to everyone and expect them to work in the same way for everyone.

They don't!

Narcissists' brains are different on a physiological level and consequently on every other level. They do not think like non-narcissistic people. They do not conduct themselves like non-narcissistic people in any type of relationship, business or personal. Nor do they respond to conflict of any sort like non-narcissistic people.

Furthermore, the people that narcissists have used and abused must be considered in a different and more compassionate way in negotiations as well. Depending on the length of their exposure to the narcissistic "manipulationship," these people truly have been traumatized and may not be in a position to think clearly.

Who needs to understand this? Well, in short, everyone. We all negotiate all day long, but not as much as the following:

Judges
Lawyers
Mediators
C-level executives
Managers
Salespeople
Arbitrators
Clergy
Psychologists, including child psychologists
All medical professionals
Parenting coordinators
Parenting/custody evaluators
Guardians ad litem
Anyone who has a toxic coworker
Anyone negotiating with a toxic family member regarding probate litigation
Anyone divorcing/divorced from a narcissist
Anyone dealing with a narcissistic co-parent (even if still in a relationship)
Anyone attempting to co-parent with a toxic ex
Anyone dealing with a narcissistic business partner

Anyone with a toxic family member

Whispers

When you are exposed to these types of tactics repeatedly, you really do start to question your own mind. You start to question your own sanity. You start to think, *Well, I don't know. Maybe I am the one who's crazy*. It really just eats away at your self-esteem, and it eats away at your sense of self, so much so that you start to question everything about yourself. You think: *Gosh, if I had just been better, if I just tried harder, if I just were more careful with my words, if…if…if…if….*

Then you spiral down into *I can prove to them that I'm worthy. It's definitely me—I'm the problem.*

There's something wrong with me.

The narcissist really has you believing all that crap.

That is…*until* you finally start to hear the whispers.

Very softly at first. Then louder and louder. Until finally, you can't ignore them anymore.

It's your soul. Your soul is speaking to you.

It's saying, "Uh-uh. This ain't right. This is not okay."

I love Maya Angelou's *I Know Why the Caged Bird Sings*, because that caged bird is your soul. When I was an attorney and people ended up in my office, or when I'm on a coaching call with somebody who's dealing with a narcissistic business partner, or I'm coaching anyone who is dealing with someone toxic and they ask me one of the *most important questions of their lives.*

"Rebecca, should I stay or should I go?"

My answer is always the same. I can't answer that for you.

The answer, dear one, lies deep within you.

You already know the answer to that question.

You're probably getting the chills when you read this passage.

I know I'm getting the chills as I type it.

The answer is deep in your gut. It's in your heart.

It's in your soul.

This is not a head decision.

This is what I call a Soul Decision.

I call it a Soul Decision, because your soul knows. Your soul knows before you do. That's what drew you to pick up this book.

Your soul knows when it's time to be free. And so, slowly but surely, you start to hear the whispers.

Slowly but surely, you see the glimpses of light start to shine through.

That's when you start watching videos like mine on YouTube or find books like these to read. Your soul gets that glimmer of light, and you go, "Oh my God, this is me. This is what's happening."

And you start gathering information, and you start getting stronger and stronger and stronger. That's when you know you're ready to start getting out of hell. How do you get your Get Out of Hell Free card? That's up next in Chapter 4.

What Can You Do Now to Start SLAYing?

1. Start using phrases to disarm the narcissist such as these:
    - "I hear/understand what you're saying."
    - "Let's discuss when you're less emotional or angry."
    - "I understand that's how you feel."
    - "Your approach is not working for me."
    - "I'm choosing not to respond to that."
    - I have so many more Key Phrases for Disarming Narcissists, which you can grab for free at www.slaythebully.com/resources

2. Start listening to the whispers in your soul and journaling what you're hearing.
3. Start creating boundaries and then be strict about them.

Mantra for Today:

I'm listening to the whispers of my soul.
(Or write one of your own that speaks to you….)

CHAPTER 4

SLAY: YOUR GET OUT OF HELL FREE CARD

"Those who escape hell never talk about it and nothing much bothers them after that."
CHARLES BUKOWSKI

When you picture hell, does it actually, maybe, possibly even sound *better* than where you are now? That's how you may feel if you've been dealing with a narcissist. If you're still reading, chances are you've found yourself in a toxic situation of your own that feels like your own fresh hell, one in which a deal with the devil may not be out of the question if it would finally provide some relief. Whether it's an abusive marriage, a soul-sucking work environment, a baneful business partnership (been there, done that—got the T-shirt), or a noxious custody battle, you've probably lost a lot of sleep over the relationship or the situation. In fact, it can take over your brain and your thoughts. You wake up in the middle of the night, and you're thinking about it. You're doing the dishes, and you're thinking about it. You're walking the dog, and you're thinking about it. You feel like you can never escape. Your life is a living hell with seemingly no way out. You don't know how you got here, but it's not good.

Most of my clients have similar stories. Having been unfairly victimized by a narcissist, they carry with them a weight of trauma from their pasts and a weight of hopelessness for the future. Then I offer them what they came for but didn't expect to find. "What if I told you there is a Get Out of Hell Free card?"

The path into hell is carefully camouflaged, concealed behind one undiscovered lie at a time, one subtle, passive-aggressive act followed by another. You do notice red flags popping up, but your attention to them is quickly diverted away through the use of artful excuses and calculated love bombs perfectly placed to keep you under the narcissist's firm control. And the narcissist does what a narcissist does best: slowly force their way into a position of power and dominance by making you feel both amazing and then inferior and deeply dependent upon them at the same time. Eventually, when the abuse is recognized, most victims don't know how to start breaking free, where to find help, or even if freedom is possible. You need to know: narcissistic abuse is a vicious cycle, but it is *one that can be broken.*

The first step is to stop blaming yourself and understand that there *is* a solution. Through my revolutionary SLAY framework, which is actually a holistic approach that blends neurolinguistic programming, traditional negotiation techniques and legal tactics, the art of persuasion of the courtroom, and some psychology, you can take back your power and walk yourself straight out of hell, with minimal burns.

Know the Playbook

The SLAY Method® is your GPS in any situation with narcissists. This can be especially comforting when the emotions turn red hot and situations are tense. It becomes difficult to think clearly and make sound decisions. Yet the paradox is that these negotiations affect the things that mean the most to us—our children, our businesses, our homes, our finances—and thus it is more critical than ever that we have a way to be able to think clearly.

Having a proven framework can be the difference between smacking down the narcissistic CEO to grab the C-level executive position you were promised when you signed on with your current company and potentially losing the job completely because you're the one who's batshit crazy. Let me explain....

This happened with one of my private coaching clients. Through working together, we were able to get out in front of the situation and save her from the "alternative" bad universe.

A total badass, Pearl had an MBA from Stanford University and a bachelor's from Harvard, and she was quite content in her position as a Chief Financial Officer living in Silicon Valley when she was contacted and strongly pursued and recruited by a private company to come work with them in Hong Kong. The Hong Kong company was part of a much larger conglomerate, all fully owned by a Swiss family worth billions, the Asian division being fully run by one of the sons. The son Charles, a handsome playboy type, flew Pearl to Hong Kong, not just once, but three times, and rolled out the red carpet for her each time. He promised her that she would be the CEO of the China portion of their corporation. While Pearl was not unhappy in her current position, the prospect of being CEO of a corporation in Asia appeared to be an excellent next step for her career.

While in Hong Kong, Charles laid it on as thick as thick can be. He was charming and personable. He was warm and inviting. He said that working for his company would be like joining a "family." Each time she visited Hong Kong, Charles asked her what her favorite foods were and made sure that he remembered every detail for restaurants. She truly felt special and welcomed each time. In her hotel room, there would be a huge welcome gift that would include flowers, food, and even a gift certificate for spa services. Charles said they always emphasized the importance of lifestyle and encouraged everyone to live healthy and balanced lives.

As for running the company itself, Pearl had questions. Charles always had the right answers. She wanted autonomy. She'd have it, he assured her. She wanted a proper marketing budget. Done, he said. In fact, he'd done his research. He knew she was environmentally conscious, and he wanted her to help them with their exhaust output so that they would be putting less toxins into the environment. He also knew that she cared deeply about women's rights, and so he suggested that when she started as CEO, she would start a women's leadership retreat, and he'd provide funding for it. She was absolutely impressed and beyond excited about all the possibilities!

Not one to make rash decisions, Pearl seriously contemplated the move. But each time she tried to potentially object to the move, Charles came back with all the reasons why she should absolutely make the move. The pressure from him was strong. He reached out to her daily. Finally, she negotiated an excellent package for herself. She looked at all the possibilities. While she didn't have kids, she did have a great husband, Joe. Pearl was Chinese but had been born in the U.S., all her family was in the United States, and Joe was American, so moving to Asia was a big deal for them. But in the end, Charles's company paid for all the relocation expenses, and Pearl was excited about her new position! She and Joe were Hong Kong-bound and she was going to be a CEO.

Almost from the moment the wheels of the airplane touched the tarmac in Hong Kong for Pearl's permanent move, there was an issue. On the first day, she arrived at the offices in Hong Kong, and Charles had his secretary show her into an office that hadn't even been fully cleaned out. There were boxes still in there that belonged to other people. Charles's manner was no longer warm and welcoming, but had turned cold and rather dismissive. He told her that there were some files that she should start to read while he attended to business that morning and that he would be able to meet with her later that morning to "catch her up." She was not introduced to anyone else in the office, nor were there business cards ready for her.

Later that day, Charles met with her and let her know that for the time being, she would be doing some busy work, until he felt she was "ready for more." He assigned a project to her and told her he wanted it completed by next week, then abruptly dismissed her from his office. There was no mention of her being CEO. Not by Charles. Not by anyone. She was not listed on the website.

The second day, Pearl returned to the office. She decided she was going to have a conversation with Charles. She asked to meet with him about the position. She was told by his secretary that he didn't have any available time that day, and that she would need to make an appointment to meet with him. Pearl scheduled time to meet with Charles. He was "unavailable" to meet with her for two more days. When they finally did meet, Charles expressed disappointment that she had started off being so "difficult" right from the beginning. He'd heard from others in the office that she had "complained" about her office, and now here she was in his office, "complaining" about her workload.

She was in disbelief!

Clearly, Pearl was not "complaining" about her workload or the office she was in, but rather, she was upset about the fact that she had a contract that clearly expressed that she was supposed to be CEO of the China division, and that was not happening. She demanded to know what was going on. He said that it was clear once she got there that she didn't have the skillset that she had represented herself as having and she needed more time to get there.

This made no sense: How would that have been "clear" on the *very first day, in the very first minute*? He hadn't even worked with her yet. And now he was labeling her as "difficult." She felt like she had stepped through Alice's looking glass.

After a few weeks, she did finally get Charles to list her on the website, but only as Interim Director of Operations for Asia. In the meantime, she did continue to receive the pay that she was promised under the terms of the contract. But the relationship with Charles grew more and more difficult. He continued to dismiss and disrespect her.

When she approached human resources with her concerns, she was shocked to learn that he had already documented her employment file, labeling her as demanding, difficult, and unprepared. She found that the other employees were also afraid of him but just didn't bother to try to say anything. They whispered about his "tantrums" and about how his family had basically given him this part of the company for "something to do."

Pearl tried contacting Charles's father to set up a meeting. She was rebuffed. Charles found out about that and exploded on her. Finally, she started Googling about narcissism and found me. That's when I started coaching her. Together we devised a plan.

When Pearl first came to me, she was shaken. While she had only been with the company about ten weeks at that time, she had already been subjected to daily narcissistic abuse by Charles. Her confidence had been stripped and she had been beaten down. She was feeling like she should have seen the signs and was being pretty hard on herself. On top of that, she was sad, hadn't slept for weeks, and was depressed, stressed, anxious, and scared to death. She was worried that if she quit, she'd never get another job. She was concerned about how it would look in the employment world to have been with a company for such a short period of time.

She was also very distressed about what Charles was going to say about her to others. Her paranoia level was high—and for good reason, frankly, given what had happened to her.

So, we developed a playbook. Once you have a playbook, then you can simply just follow it. It becomes your security blanket. Now you simply follow the map.

We used the SLAY Method® to the T. In the next several chapters, you're going to find out what that means. Through several one-on-one sessions, she and I devised a plan that incorporated a Strategy for where she wanted to go (her Vision) and the step-by-step Action Plan to get there, then we devised our Leverage, which would specifically persuade Charles to want to get to the resolution Pearl wanted (again, her Vision), all while Anticipating how he would behave along the way, staying two steps ahead of him, and continuing to focus on Pearl's side of the equation. It worked like a charm!

Pearl ended up getting the buyout package she wanted. She ended up starting her own business, and today she is thriving.

Pearl Team Smackdown Rules!

Having a secure plan can also be the difference between realizing you can achieve freedom and staying in and habitually returning to an abusive situation with your malignant narcissistic husband or business partner.

One of my clients didn't have a plan to escape her abusive then-husband. She had tried once but wasn't quite ready, and so it didn't work, and unfortunately, she had to go crawling back to him. He started off by saying he'd "changed." They went to therapy. He even convinced the therapist he'd changed.

But eventually she realized he hadn't changed. He'd only gotten worse. Then he wanted her to suffer for having left him, and he was far worse than he'd been before.

Finally, she decided to leave *again*. But this time she devised a plan. She had private conversations with her family, who would help her secure funds to find a place to stay for a few months. She took her husband off all her credit card accounts, put herself on her mother's checking account, didn't tell anyone where she was going, packed a bag, and took off in the middle of the night. This time she was leaving for good. Once she had a plan, she was able to execute it.

Every narcissist expects to get what they want, but the game changes once you decide what *you* want and realize you can get it. Now that you have a strong mindset, you need a strong Strategy to move forward.

The SLAY Method®

In Chapter 1, I introduced you to the SLAY Method®. Over the next several chapters, I will be going much deeper into the specifics of each of the areas of the SLAY Method®—Strategy, Leverage, Anticipation, and You.

My client Peter, who I told you about in Chapter 3, who went up against both his wife *and* his mother and won, said, "My case was probably the worst there was. While it was hard to see it while going through it, to anyone going through it, I now say, stay positive and stay strong. There's light at the end of the tunnel. I'm stronger. I'm wiser and knowledgeable and grateful. There's nothing I can't do. No matter what comes at me in life. I feel like a rock. I'm proud of that. I'm proud to be on the other side of it now. I feel like I can conquer anything!"

But First, Fear

> "I became this shell of a woman. This shell of who I once was. Any security I once had, any knowledge I once had, I felt was gone. I had this dream, that pipeline dream, that we were going to be married forever [with] multiple kids—all of it. And I think if I could best describe it, fear took over my brain, like I couldn't even rationalize anything, anything. Anything. Like, I was actually on my hands and knees, like the walls were closing in on me. I mean, it was like I was suffocating. Because of the fear. Because of the situation, and the heartache. And [I was] just totally overwhelmed. And drained."
>
> Laila

Laila's words so aptly describe how so many people feel at the end of a relationship with a narcissist, and I'm so grateful that my SLAY Method® helped her. Even if you're in a non-romantic relationship with a narcissist, the feelings can be quite similar to a romantic relationship. I often teach live masterclasses to people who have been dealing with narcissists in all walks of life, from business partners to bosses, family members to exes, co-parents, and anything in between. For those of us who've dealt with the pain of narcissistic abuse, we feel so isolated, so ashamed, so alone, and as if no one else understands, but once you realize that: 1) narcissists are so similar to each other, and 2) the pain that other targets are feeling too is so similar to what you're experiencing, it is so comforting. The path to healing becomes so much clearer once you know what you're dealing with.

I want you to hear, in real-world words, how others have described what the hell, the fear, of dealing with a narcissist was like:

> *I felt paralyzed, like anything I was going to say was going to be foolish or just plain wrong.*
>
> —Max, medical doctor dealing with his narcissistic boss

> *I can't sleep at night thinking of what might happen.*
>
> —Neil, realtor dealing with a narcissistic ex

> *I'm afraid everyone is going to believe his lies.*
>
> —Sarah, entrepreneur dealing with a narcissistic ex

> *I feel bullied, and not sure if I should speak up, and if so when, or how.*
>
> —Amanda, CEO of PR Company, dealing with narcissistic client(s)

> *I'm so afraid that I feel like I have scrambled eggs for brains.*
>
> —Cindy, homemaker of thirty years dealing with a narcissistic ex

> *I am so afraid of backlash that I don't want to do anything at all.*
>
> —Angela, actress dealing with narcissistic a ex/co-parent

> *I constantly feel like I'm walking on eggshells. I just don't want anything to blow up in my face, or my kids' faces.*
>
> —Christian, engineer dealing with a narcissistic ex

Sound familiar?

Here's the paradox. Narcissists make you feel like you are walking on eggshells because they feel fear. They are deathly afraid. They are deathly afraid of being abandoned, of being alone, of being exposed, of rejection, of humiliation, of their own failure, and the list goes on.

Here's the way I see shifting the paradigm of power with narcissists: it's as if you are righting a ship's course of direction—or making a full U-turn. You're turning around a massive yacht or cruise ship, but the first thing you have to do is stop the thing from going in the direction it's been traveling in. You can't turn it around until you stop it first.

You've already started the process. The next thing to realize is that the only way out is through. Unfortunately, there will be no George Jetson spaceships flying in to save you by picking you up and flying you away. You'll have to endure it. But if it's any consolation, I heard the best analogy once about growth: to build muscle, you have to first create little tears in the fibers of the muscle. When the body repairs those tears, those muscles are then more adaptable and prepared to handle what caused the "damage" in the first place. Thus, the muscles are now stronger. We are like those muscles. What doesn't kill us makes us stronger, right?

When I first got divorced, my kids were so little, and I was still in my twenties. I put myself through law school at night, and I was teaching inner-city elementary school during the day. My life was such chaos. I remember saying to my mom, "I wish I could freeze my kids over here, clean up my life, finish law school, and then go back and get them!" Well obviously, life doesn't work like that! My first three kids and I all powered through together. The only way out is through. We made it, and so will you.

Once you stop the conditioning, the next step is to feel strong enough to start to walk forward in the other direction, but just gently enough so that the narcissist doesn't realize there's a new game in town. This new dynamic is one in which you no longer back down. This is where the narcissist starts to feel the shift in the winds. You don't do this all at once, but on your own time. When you're ready.

Finally, you'll start to feel strong enough to truly negotiate powerfully on your own behalf. You'll be able to walk forward powerfully and confidently and not backward. You'll sleep at night and not think about what any narcissist is going to do. You'll know you've conquered not just narcissists, but your own fears.

With regard to fear of negotiating, or fear in general, I had to come to terms with the fact that in some areas of my life, *it's not ever going away entirely*.

Instead, whenever I feel fear, I have learned to have a conversation with it. It's a modification of a conversation I read that Elizabeth Gilbert, the author of *Eat, Pray, Love*, has with herself when she starts to write, because she still struggles with fear around writing. I have sort of changed it up for myself. Feel free to do the same for yourself.

Mine sounds like this:

> "*Fear, you and I are going on a ride together. I would like for you to not come along. But I realize that's not possible. I realize you're coming, so I guess you can come. But you have to sit in the back seat. You definitely do* **not** *get to pick the music. You definitely do* **not** *get to talk. And* **most** *importantly, you do* **not** *get to touch the steering wheel!*"

Basically, the idea is that you understand that fear is never going away entirely. You and fear are going to have to find a way to peacefully coexist without it dominating you and paralyzing you. It does not get to control you.

Michael Singer, author of *The Untethered Soul*, likens fear to a "thing." Regarding fear, he says you really only have two choices, which are to try to push it away or let it pass through you. If you try to push it away, then you're going to have this arduous journey, because you're going to try to "control" situations so that you don't ever have to feel the fear. The problem is that you'll still always be feeling it. The second option allows you to relax and "harmonize" with fear. By doing this, Singer says, "[y]ou learn how to interface and interact with life in a wholesome, participatory way. Letting go of fear is not letting go of life."

Strength Training

Whether your relationship is strictly professional, personal, or deeply personal, any relationship with a narcissist can be compared to a parasitic relationship. That's why they are sometimes referred to as Energy Vampires. Once the host rips that supply from them, the parasite ain't happy. Nope. Not at all.

The great news is that on the other side of this thing is the best version of you that ever lived, and it will totally be worth it. Totally. Trust me.

Mary was a great example.

With her short, cropped hair, cardigan sweaters, and plain face, Mary seemed more like a Catholic nun from Ohio than the wife of a Middle Eastern surgeon, who also happened to hold the patent for one of the most lucrative orthopedic surgical inventions. A kind woman in her sixties, her husband often baselessly accused her of leering at other men in elevators and would then make her "pay" for it for days with abusive behavior, sometimes just verbal and sometimes worse. She decided she'd had enough long before she finally had the strength to leave.

She came to consult with me, then spent the next several years slowly gathering financial documents. She gathered the financial documents in bits and pieces that she was going to need for the divorce, such as bank statements, credit statements, and income tax statements. These are all the types of documents that the court will need to have an accurate depiction of what is his, what is hers, and what is theirs at the end of the day. She'd then stop into my office and drop off what she'd found every few months. As she gathered the documents, she also gathered her strength and her nerve.

Throughout the divorce process, she was shaky and felt crazy, and he was threatening. But by the time the divorce was over many years later, Mary was a totally different person. She was outgoing, socializing, wearing her hair longer, wearing makeup, and exuding confidence. The coolest!

The horrible thing about trying to leave a narcissist is that they are probably going to flip out. They just are. But you can take it. We will cover a lot more of this in the "A" section—Anticipate—and how to deal with it so you'll be ready. I do want to mention here that if you ever feel that you are in any sort of danger of physical abuse, and you live in the United States, please contact the National Domestic Violence Hotline at 1-800-799-7233.

I think of their behavior as like a toddler who has a tantrum on the floor. If the parent gives in, then the next time, the toddler knows that they just must scream louder and longer, and the parent will eventually give in. That's what's going on with the narcissist. They figure that they'll just scream louder and longer, and eventually you'll give in. You're basically just doing the Ferber method with them. For those of you who are parents, you may remember doing that with your babies. The pediatrician's advice was to ignore their crying, hoping the babies would eventually fall asleep "on their own." In the case of narcissists, you must ignore them, in the hopes that they will eventually just fade off and find a different source of supply.

To enter any negotiations and gain a mental, emotional, and spiritual advantage, your mindset will have to be powerful, so making sure that you practice self-care throughout the entire time that you're negotiating with the narcissist is not only recommended, but highly critical. The drama, trauma, and chaos will be heightened and continuous. If you are heading into a court battle, it will be even worse.

Seeking professional and outside advice, receiving counsel, and recruiting helpful allies, such as trustworthy friends, family members, counselors, and mentors, can help you to see the situation from a different perspective. Receiving feedback, wisdom, and encouragement from an honest and unbiased voice is transformative in shifting your view, being reminded of what you deserve, and renewing your confidence.

But of course, *other people* cannot always be with you. In those cases, you will have to fold in self-care. I will focus a lot more on this in Chapter 8, the You section, but this is so important that

I want to mention it here also. To be strong, you must take care of yourself.

Here are some ways you can start to do that now:

1. **Pivot**: I very much try to not let these people rent too much free space in my head, but obviously sometimes that doesn't work. When you start going down that dark, dark alley in the bad, bad neighborhood of focusing on poisonous thoughts like *I can't believe this person didn't see all that I gave to them, I can't believe they didn't see what a good person I was, I gave all of this and they still wanted more,* or *I can't believe that they would treat me this way after all I did for them,* it can be very hard to find your way out. I call it being in "Victim Mode."

   You definitely want to "pivot" out of that place as soon as you can, because being stuck there means being stuck in one super dangerous neighborhood for sure. If you're in Victim Mode, then you can't be in Creation Mode. You can't be in Confidence Mode. You certainly can't be in Power Mode to negotiate with narcissists, and you can't be in the Getting-to-the-Rest-of-Your-Life Mode. Plus, remember: like attracts like. That means those negative thoughts you're having are going to bring more bad juju into your life. No thank you. That's why, as fast as you can, you want to pivot out of that neighborhood.

   This is when I say, "Deal with the narcissists when they are in front of your face, but other than that, do not spend any more time on thinking about them." I know: easier said than done.

But when you find yourself thinking about them, pivot. Find something else that you can pivot directly to. It's easier if you have something that you know you are going to pivot to directly.

For example, one of my friends decided she was going to write a new book, another friend decided she was going to create a support group and spend time on that, and another friend decided to go back to school. Another idea is to have a variety of activities at the ready, such as planning your vacation, then moving into starting to write that book you've always to write, or whatever. Just have something else at the ready right away after that is over. Choose anything that will help you shift your mind away from thinking about the negative energy of that person.

You want to create something that you know that you will be able to pivot to thinking about right away, instead of the narcissist, so that when anything happens with the narcissist, you have something else that is positive to immediately direct your attention to instead. You want it to be something that you are excited about and something that will lift your spirits and your energy.

2. **Meditate**. Meditating, even for just a few minutes a day, is scientifically proven to start changing your neuronal patterns. It can start to change your breathing. Sometimes when we're so stressed, we don't even realize that we're not even taking enough oxygen into our bodies. Just taking a few deep breaths in will refresh the cells in our bodies, give them oxygen, and give us more energy.

If you haven't meditated at all before, try this. Sit still or lay down. Then picture, as you're inhaling, that you are taking in positive energy, and as you are exhaling, that you are just releasing all that negative energy and that negative tension. Try setting your phone for one minute to start. Then work your way up to five minutes or more a day. It'll make a huge difference for you.

There are also apps out there if you want help with this, and there are even YouTube videos that can help you with meditating too. There are meditation classes online as well. You could also even find a place that has a meditation class near your home if you have the time and resources to attend in person. (My cousin found his one true love in a meditation class when he was in his sixties, so you never know what could happen!)

3. **Find Your Vibe Tribe**. By raising the vibrational energy of the people that you spend time with, you also raise your own vibrational energy. Don't spend time with people who bring you down. We all have vibrational energy. It's measurable. This is a law of physics. This is not a woo-woo thing. If you are with people who are sad, depressed, bringing you down, or just simply not supportive of you, it will cause you to feel darker.

   The poet Rumi said, "Set your life on fire. Seek those who fan your flames." Be with people who want to throw logs on your fire and help it grow. You can tell if someone is on your side. You can feel it in your gut. Start being really choosy about who gets to be in your space. Alternatively, are the people you are surrounding yourself with trying to put your fire out by throwing water on it? If that's what's happening, then it's time to find another group of people to be with, because those aren't friends. Even if they're family, give yourself permission to limit the amount of time you spend with them. Think about how you feel after you've been with them. Do you feel lighter and more joyful? Or is there a pit in your gut?

Your soul always knows.

4. **Oxygenate to Dominate**. Get some oxygen into those cells by moving around a little bit. It's time to exercise. If you do not have any sort of exercise routine now, then you can start small. Commit to walking around the block twice a day or going to a yoga class. There are yoga classes offered online as well as on YouTube. Do anything that will get your juices flowing.

   Science shows that there are many neurological health benefits to exercise, including stress reduction and improved memory, and it can help with inflammation as well. There is nothing more stressful in the world than dealing with narcissists. Long-term exposure to stress can lead to all sorts of physical problems such as higher cortisol levels, which can lead to diabetes, weight gain, fatigue, muscle weakness, intestinal issues, and even autoimmune diseases.

   Maybe even find an accountability partner so that it makes it a bit more fun. That way you're more likely to do it, and you have someone to support you in the process.

Choose whichever self-care routine works for you. If none of these resonate, then find something else. Just pick something. You will need something as you go through this process. Being in a relationship with a narcissist was difficult. Getting out of the relationship will take every ounce of strength you can muster too. But as I said, it's worth it, and you can do it.

Then, Believe, Believe, Believe

I will repeat this theme here several times throughout this book, because, yes, it's that important. Mindset is everything—90 percent of winning begins before you even walk into the room. If you don't believe you can win, no one can help you. You don't need a good lawyer, a good book, good facts, nothing. None of that will help you if you don't believe you can win.

You must believe it first.

Only then will everything else line up for you.

There will be times when it will get hard to continue to believe. I have heard the ill-fated lines. Here are some examples:

> *Everyone always believes the narcissist's lies.*
>
> *There's no point in trying to negotiate with narcissists.*
>
> *The system is skewed.*
>
> *The narcissist always wins (or gets away with everything). The judges (or mediators, custody evaluators, or parenting coordinators) are biased.*
>
> *The ________________ (judge, mediator, parenting evaluator) doesn't like me, because the narcissist told them lies about me and charmed them.*

Honestly, the list here could be endless. It doesn't matter.

So, here's a question for you. Do you want to be right about all these things above? If so, where does that get you? Woo-hoo. Congratulations. You're right! Go you! And now what?

Or? How about we decide that things can be different?

I've had cases where it seemed all throughout the case that the judge was completely against my client, and then in the end, we won everything. You just have to believe it can happen.

Remember that quote attributed to Henry Ford: "Whether you think you can or can't, you're right." I know this to be true. There are so many stories of visionaries such as Steve Jobs, Thomas Edison, or the Wright Brothers who simply didn't listen to "reason" but just decided that they were going to have a particular outcome. They just said to themselves, "This is how this is going." You can too. From here on out, you must believe that success is your only option.

Period.

The *only* way to do that? Build a Super Strong Strategy. That's your foundation. That's what we do next in Chapter 5.

What Can You Do Now to Start SLAYing?

1. Decide how you're going to process the fear as it comes through you.
2. Decide which of the self-care routines you will start to incorporate in your daily life:
    - Pivot
    - Meditate
    - Find Your Vibe Tribe
    - Oxygenate to Dominate

3. Believe that you can win.

   Create statements that you believe—and place them in places where you will see them often, such on the lock screen of your phone, the home screen of your computer, or on sticky notes that you place on your bathroom mirror—such as "I believe I will win" or "I believe I can have the outcome that I want." Or choose an "I believe" statement that resonates with you.

Mantra for Today:

I am a winner.
(Or write one of your own that speaks to you....)

CHAPTER 5

S: STRATEGY: A STRONG FOUNDATION EQUALS BREAKTHROUGH RESULTS

"If you're going through hell, keep going."
WINSTON CHURCHILL

The first step, the S in SLAY, is developing your Super Strong Strategy. This is your foundation and your GPS for your entire negotiation. Many people want to skip right to L—creating Leverage—but if you don't make sure to implement your Leverage under the plan of a Strategy, then it will be a complete waste of time. You'll be twisting in the wind and may not end up where you want to be.

What is that you want at the end of the day? What do you want the outcome of your negotiations to be? You need to be able to keep your eye on the prize.

There are two major steps to developing a powerful Strategy. First you create your Vision. This provides direction when you aren't sure what path to take or what decisions to make. Your Vision then informs the framework for your Action Plan. The Action Plan is where you create the steps you will take towards your Vision. Between your Vision and your Action Plan, you are creating a solution to your problem.

There's one thing I want to make sure I say right here and now. In my life, I have gone to law school with three babies as a single mom in my twenties, while still working as a teacher in public school, and made Law Review (which was the highest honor in law school and based upon my grades). I also created a multi-million-dollar law firm, then merged that practice. Then I moved on and created a brand-new online business, which now serves millions of people all over the world. I tell you all of this to say this one thing: I know what makes a person successful. Vision, planning, and then *execution* of that Action Plan.

Just start doing it. Even if you don't feel ready or like you have all the tools in your pocket yet, once you have your Vision and your Action Plan, the cool thing about it is that it's right in front of you, and all you have to do is start moving on it. Just start executing it.

The only difference between people who are successful and people who are not is one word: execution. Just start. You can do this. I love the John Burroughs quote "Leap and the net will appear." Remember I am here with you, guiding you in this journey every step of the way.

Creating a winning Vision and then deciding that that is how it is happening even in the face of what feels like the most crushing circumstances is absolutely the most powerful factor deciding your outcome.

Before we get into how to create your Vision and your Action Plan, though, I do want to give you a few cautions that take place at the beginning of negotiations.

Cautions for the Beginning of Negotiations!

It's Go time. Time to get ready to start to negotiate with a narcissist.

Now, because I've done this a time or two—or a thousand (or more)—please listen carefully to me. And listen good and hard.

Are my words penetrating your brain? I have your attention? Yes? Okay, good.

Here's how the negotiations will look at the beginning.

YOU will say (very naively) something to the effect of, "I only want what's fair, and I don't want to fight." But *you* will *actually mean it.*

The narcissist will absolutely say something like that too. *To your face.* You will believe them. But it will be a bald-faced, down and dirty, hairy, massive lie.

Remember narcissists fight dirty. They are street fighters. Remember when I said that if this were an actual physical fight, they would be pulling your hair, biting your ear, and kicking you in the groin, all while you are saying you don't want to fight?

Whether it's a business, probate, or divorce negotiation, the rules for negotiation in regular situations just aren't necessarily the same here. Yes, there are many things that do apply to all negotiations. Yes, both sides want to feel seen and heard and know that they matter. Yes, you need to do your research for both sides. But there are some very critical parts to dealing with narcissists that are just quite bluntly not universal.

You may think (also very naively) that by being generous up front, you will somehow garner favor, that the narcissist will see how reasonable you're being, and respond to that accordingly by also being reasonable. They will not.

Here's a perfect example. When I interviewed Dr. Joe Vitale, bestselling author who was also featured in the movie

The Secret, he was just finishing a two-and-a-half-year divorce, and he said:

> "This divorce should have been over easily and effortlessly, because what I offered was basically the world—because I was willing to walk away. What happened instead is that the 'narcissistic' other side decided to create a persecution of my life and business, and it has been the most excruciating, tortuous, emotionally exhaustive, expensive, painful experience of my entire life. Including when I was homeless and including when I was in poverty."

What will really happen is that you will give away all sorts of potential leverage by being "generous" and "fair" at the beginning to show how "reasonable" you're being. You will do this because that's who you are. If you haven't read this book and realized that their brains are different from your brain, and cannot process things the way that yours does, you might think, *Well, why would they want to waste time, money, and energy on this thing? Of course, they want to come to a conclusion.*

Well, of course you now know the answer to that.

So let me save you a lot of time, money, and headache right now.

Most of the time, what ends up happening is this. You will float out all sorts of generous ways to resolve your issues—ways that are more than fair—but then nothing whatsoever will be resolved. But the narcissist will then want to hold you to those offers that you floated out there, as if they were agreements that you *actually made*, but then not give you anything in return.

Even worse than that, sometimes they lure you into signing something early on. Then you really end up feeling helpless, used, and abused.

All of this ends up as just an exercise that leaves you feeling frustrated and like you've gotten nowhere before you even really began. Plus, and this is the worst part, you may end up giving away leverage that you probably shouldn't have right away. (Much more on this in the leverage chapter coming up next).

There are also a few tricks that narcissists pull right at the beginning of negotiations that you need to be aware of (or beware of), especially if you are going through a divorce, but in other areas too:

1. The narcissist may try to get you to sign something or just enter into any sort of agreement early on, without you really knowing everything you need to know. For example, if it is a divorce action, you might need to know the value of a business, what the balances are in certain accounts, or what the appraised values are of certain pieces of real estate. They might tell you that you don't need to know any of that and that you can just sign an agreement without that information. They may bully you into signing something by getting you to agree to meet at Starbucks or somewhere else without a lawyer.
2. If you are going through a divorce, the narcissist may suggest a "collaborative" approach at the beginning. This is where you engage two collaborative attorneys and try to work it out amicably, but if it doesn't get resolved, then you have to fire those lawyers and hire two completely different lawyers and start all over. Warning: the collaborative approach *will not* work with a true narcissist.

Don't waste your money. It will wind up being much more expensive.

3. If you are going through a divorce, the narcissist may try to discredit your lawyer right away. They do this to drive a wedge between you and the new person who might have control over you, as they want to be the one who maintains control over you. Here are some of the things they may say:

   "Your lawyer just wants your money."
   "You don't need a lawyer. We can do this ourselves."
   "You don't need a separate lawyer. I already have one, and we can use the same one." (This is not true. Lawyers can only represent one person at a time.)
   "Your lawyer has too many cases."
   "Your lawyer is lying to you about me/what I said. I'm telling you the truth."

Now, here is what I want to say to you. I have had to have this talk with some of my clients also. You know the narcissist is a liar. You tell everyone you know that the narcissist is a liar. Why on God's Earth would they be telling you the truth about this particular thing? Especially when they know that this person is being brought in to help you to potentially work against them? Yet the narcissist is often so swift and cunning at love bombing, they can lure their targets right back where they want them to be during this phase.

Let me tell you guys: *you are in the discard phase here. You are Public Enemy Number One.* Unless you're planning to stay in a relationship with this person, which we already determined is *highly not recommended* (like, if surgeon generals could issue warnings about them being a serious risk to your health, they should), then you cannot believe anything they say!

Newsflash: everything they do is manipulation! If they apologize, it is a manipulation. If they say they will change—manipulation. If they say they want to resolve the issues amicably—manipulation.

A Word about Choosing a Lawyer:

> Make sure you choose someone who you trust and feel has your back. You don't want to feel traumatized twice and as if you need to defend yourself to your own attorney. You also want to establish a relationship of trust and communication with your attorney. In my SLAY program, I do have Questions for Vetting Attorneys, and I also have a packet for sharing with your attorney. I also have websites for finding attorneys within the program. Much more on my website at www.slaythebully.com/resources.

Once the narcissist realizes that you aren't buying into their "do everything my way" and "give me everything" games (and oh, by the way, it still won't be over even after that), then it will be game on. Watch the mask *whip off.*

You'd better be on the defensive and vigilant. All. Of. The. Time.

The narcissist's injury will have been triggered, causing the narcissistic rage to come flying out. They feel threatened, and you are potentially taking away one of their major supply sources—*you.*

They are *not* happy about giving up a source of supply.

Maybe I'm jaded because I have been dealing with narcissists for so long. But at the start of regular negotiations, when non-narcissistic people are on each side, both sides are fresh-faced, clear-headed, and eager to find common ground, because both sides want to find a place where resolution is the outcome. Both sides realize that they don't want to waste time or money, so they look for ways to come to an effective resolution.

That is not the case here.

At the start of the negotiation where there is a narcissist on one side, depending upon how long you've been dealing with the narcissist and what your relationship has been, your head is not clear. You are likely depleted—mentally, physically, emotionally, and spiritually. You feel like you have done nothing but defend yourself, sometimes for years. You may have c-PTSD.

You have felt like you've been beat up for so long that you're just completely and utterly depleted. The narcissist has no interest in coming to a resolution at all, because they are enjoying the process of making the other person miserable, because they get narcissistic supply from it.

I distinctly remember this dialog from the start of a divorce mediation years ago—this was long before I knew what a narcissist was or what narcissistic supply was. Looking back, it is now so glaringly obvious. Take a look:

> **Mediator** [during his opening conversation to both husband and wife]: Today is a day of opportunity. If you resolve your case today, you can do it in private, and it will save you thousands of dollars in attorneys' fees. Plus, you can resolve in any way that you want, and it isn't appealable. Your case can be over today. This is a really great opportunity for you both to get your case over

with today in your way. [Turning to wife] Would you like to get your case settled today?

Wife: Yes, I would.

Mediator [to husband]: Would you like to get your case settled today?

Husband [folding his arms over his chest, then looking forward and speaking angrily in a huff]: Nope!

Mediator [to husband]: You wouldn't? Why not?

Husband: Personal reasons.

This meant he just wanted to continue to make the wife's life miserable, which is exactly what he did for many months to come.

Thus, you must have a Vision, and you have to have a quest for that Vision. And you must have a will to win for that Vision. It has to be more powerful and steelier than anything you have ever felt in your life.

The Power of Decision and Vision

Initially, creating Strategy (including your own Vision) may feel foreign to you, because you may feel like you've been a turtle on your back for so long, meaning that you've been defending yourself constantly, and so it hasn't occurred to you to even think about what it is that you actually want. But if you don't figure out what you want and where you're going, then you can't get there.

Once you realize that you can create a Vision, then see it actually come to fruition before your eyes, that's when your life truly transforms.

But before you create that Vision, there's actually another step, and that step is to *decide* what that Vision is going to be.

Then you can create a powerful Vision.

Let me tell you a story of how this worked in my own life.

I mentioned that I was dealing with a narcissistic business partner who was driving me crazy. A few years ago, I merged my law practice with two other guys and decided to branch out into other business ventures. I knew I was more of an entrepreneur at heart.

In one of those endeavors, I had just gotten the company started when this person came along. I met her through other professionals that I already knew. She seemed to have great credentials and of course had all the charm and charisma and was seemingly intelligent. Right away, she showed a heavy interest in my project, first with how supportive she was, but then by emailing me daily with how she could bring in amazing connections. Then she started telling me that for her to really bring them in, her name needed to be on my project publicly.

That took me aback, but then she started promising that she could get me massive speaking engagements including keynotes, but once again, she really wanted to be named publicly as a partner in my new endeavor. She offered to throw in half the expenses, and that seemed enticing to me, so while my gut was telling me it wasn't a good idea, I went ahead and did it. We celebrated with dinner and champagne. I barely knew her, but it would be great, I told myself, *right?*

But once I put her name on it—everything changed right away.

Her amazing contacts—none of them materialized.

She would promise to do things for the business, then just not follow through, but become passive-aggressive and then lie and say she had done the things she hadn't done.

She would lie to me and to others.

Then there were times when I even caught her lying about money. She had deposited business money into her personal account instead of the business account.

She was also lying about me to clients and to third parties. She would put me down in front of third parties during meetings as well as take credit for work I had done.

I started to become paranoid, wondering what she was going to do next, lie about next, say next. I became obsessed. Those old feelings of being bullied as a child were being triggered. I found myself saying nothing many times and allowing her to get away with a lot of it. I wasn't sure what to say, or how to approach it.

It was a very different situation than when I was dealing with people as their attorney. Standing up for others—that I could do all day long. But when it came time to stand up for myself, once again I found myself without a voice.

It was during this time that my family and I went on an amazing dream vacation to Maui, Hawaii. One of the excursions that you can do there is get up at crazy o'clock in the morning and drive up the mountain of Haleakalā and see the sunrise. When one of our friends suggested we do this, I thought they were nuts.

You literally get up at like 2:30 a.m., then drive from where it is eighty-five degrees to a few hours up the mountain to watch the sunrise, where it is like forty degrees. I am a person who hates to get up that early and hates cold weather. But I'm telling you, this is something you must add to your bucket list if you've never done it. The sunrise is spectacular. It is literally heaven on Earth.

I was there with my husband and my youngest daughter. People whom I love.

The sunrise was stunning to behold. A Hawaiian man began to chant to revere the sun as it was coming up. Even my daughter, who was seventeen at the time, leaned forward to me and whispered, "Mom, it's Heaven on Earth."

"Yes, yes, it is" I responded.

Ahhh, I should have been thinking. *I'm on vacation. I'm with the people that I love the most.* It should have been a moment of pure bliss.

But I wasn't thinking of that moment of bliss. What was I thinking of at that moment?

Yup. You guessed it. The narcissist.

And then it hit me.

I suddenly thought, *No. No. No! You don't get to be here!*

It's one thing to obsess about toxic things or people when I'm working or walking around and living my regular life. But on my vacation, in Heaven on Earth? Oh no. This was not okay.

At that moment, something shifted for me.

The person who went up that mountain was not the person who went down that mountain.

Because I made a decision.

I want you all to know the power of a decision. The Deciding Factor. Do you know what the root of the word "decide" is?

It is *cide*, from the Latin for *to kill* or *to cut off*.

When you *decide* on a path, the universe, God, Allah, Love, the Creator, whatever you believe, all start lining up for you to cheer you on.

I want you all to know the power of choice. It is a redemptive power. It is magic.

I realized in that moment on the mountain that I had a choice! I realized if I was thinking about the narcissist, I was allowing myself to be a victim. I was not using my life to be a creator. I realized I was not being a victor.

I decided to create a vision. I decided that rather than focusing on a relationship that wasn't serving me, I would do something that would use my gifts. I decided to finish the negotiation book I had already started months before.

I went back home and created a plan. Within a few weeks, the book was completed. It went on to become an Amazon number-one bestseller when it was published and continues to perform well to this day. It all started with the decision to create a powerful Vision.

Creating Your Vision

When you create your Vision, get super specific. This will become your North Star. This is your end goal, the outcome you are working toward. I also like to refer to your Vision as your guiding policy, although some may think that phrase sounds a little bit like we are about to create something for the government. While I joke, it actually really can guide you along the way and keep your focus where it needs to be, especially when you get triggered (which you will) and when you feel like giving up (and that may happen too, unfortunately). You will know where you're going. You will be able to keep your eyes on the prize.

What will be your Vision? What is that you actually want? Many times, when I am doing one-on-one coaching with clients, this is the hardest question for people. When they've been dealing with a narcissist for so long, a lot of times they've just been in defense mode. It hasn't even occurred to them to think about what they want.

Remember the purpose of your Vision is to give you direction when you're not certain what decisions to make while the negotiations are actively going or when you have to communicate with the narcissist. It is where you will be channeling all your choices, to give them context. This will become the filter and lens through which everything will flow.

Before You Start...Remember That Negative Thoughts Will Never Lead to a Positive Life

It is very critical here that you determine what is most important to you, and that it's *not* anything that has to do with the narcissist. What I mean by that is, for example, exacting revenge on the narcissist is not a sound Vision. What we are working toward for you is an outcome that is positive, for your life and for the future that you are creating and living. Having a Vision that is based in revenge will not serve you in the long run.

First, Brainstorm Everything That Is Most Important to You

Make a list. Write down everything, but in no particular order. Just get it all out on paper. Once you've done that, then take a look at what you've written down. You may even want to take those items and put them on notecards to make them easier to move around. Now start prioritizing. Which of these is most important to you?

Also, look at all aspects of your life. To help give you context, I would think of it in terms of the most critical areas that we all have as humans. They are:

Mental
Physical
Financial
Relational
Spiritual

Obviously, your overall goal or goals do not have to include all the above, but you can consider each one of them and then decide which ones you need to include in your Vision.

Many people use the word "goals." The reason I don't love the word "goal" is that personally I feel like a goal is something you're always striving for but never quite achieve. To me, a Vision is something you actually see and then achieve. There is an actual outcome attached to it.

Second, Write Out Each Outcome You Want and If Appropriate, When You Want to Achieve Each Outcome By

In other words, if you could design the perfect outcome, what would that look like? Make it as specific as possible, including when you would like to see it happen. Write your desired outcomes out in list format. Here are some prompts for helping you figure out your perfect outcome:

1. By three months from now, I want ________________
2. This is going to be the outcome: ________________
   by ____
3. My perfect Vision is ____________________________

A Word About Words

Words matter. Your words create your reality. Be very, very careful with your words. Do not say things like "I will try to do it. I will do it if I can." As Yoda said, "Do or do not. There is no try." Use "I am" statements, such as "I am powerful" or "I am creative." Or if those don't feel right just yet, then say, "I am feeling better every day" or "I know I am on the right path." Be very aware of your words. Your words are placing orders with the Universe.

Third, Figure Out Your "Why" for Each Statement

Once you have created your Vision Statements, I want you to decide why you want them. I want you to really get present with the feelings you have about your Visions, why they are so important to you, and how you will feel when you have the outcome that you desire.

There is a science behind why the emotional aspect is so very important. Once you put your energy and power into your Vision, nothing can stop you. But you truly must believe in it. You must know why you want to achieve your outcomes. You have to feel them with all your might and with every single cell in your body. This is where the magic really starts to happen for you.

If you don't, then when the narcissist comes along and gets you rattled, you will be shaken and want to give up. You will forget what it is that you are doing. You may be taken back in by what the narcissist says once again or be pressured to do things you don't want to do in the negotiations. But if you believe in your heart and soul that you will be able to achieve the Vision that you have created, once you have set that intention, nothing can stop you.

While many call this the Law of Attraction, there actually is scientific data behind this. Without getting too technical, let's just put it this way: your thoughts are beams of energy. When you think a thought, you are emitting that thought out into space, and since it is a quantum law of physics that when energies of the same vibrations align, they are attracted to each other, meaning "like attracts like," you are literally attracting exactly what you think into your space.

Your thoughts, via your emotions, are the most powerful forms of energy and can even be measured in hertz, which are energy units of frequency. The better you feel, the higher your vibrational frequency. I will talk more about this in Chapter 10. For now, know that putting your why behind your Vision will help you to achieve your outcome so much faster. Here are some prompts you can use to help you figure out your why:

1. It is most important to me because ____________
2. I want this because ____________
3. I am motivated to have this because ____________
4. This is my mission because ____________
5. This is my "why" because ____________

Now it's time to put all three steps together. There really is no right or wrong in creating your Vision Statements. They will be as unique as you are. Next, we will be creating your Action Plan. Throughout the process, your Action Plan may change, but your Vision Statements shouldn't change all that much. When something happens that you have to respond to, when you have to make a decision, or when you are interacting with the narcissist, you will be running everything through your Visions by asking yourself, *If I respond in this way, will it serve my Visions? Does it get me closer to that end?* If it does, then you move forward with that action; if it does not, then you do not.

Take some time right now to create your Vision Statements. Here are some sample Vision Statements:

> *To have, within six months, a settlement that is fair under the law and allows me to move on in peace.*
>
> *To receive enough financially for me to be able to move forward by June 1 and start my new life.*
>
> *To negotiate an equitable outcome by the end of the year and still feel in flow.*
>
> *To have an end result that allows me to feel whole and complete within three months and have no regrets in the process.*

Action Plan

Now it's time to create your Action Plan. When you go into action, you go from paralysis and analysis to grooving and moving. If you've been in a relationship with a narcissist, I want you to think about it this way: you are course correcting. Depending upon how long you've been in the relationship with the narcissist, you've been love bombed, devalued, and discarded so many times that you don't know which way is up sometimes. You've been walking backwards and defending yourself over and over and over. I think of the picture in this way: your ship has been moving backwards. Now, though, you are going to want to turn it all the way around, 180 degrees, and start heading in the other direction, toward the narcissist—to start fighting back. You're the one going on the offensive for a change, and feeling not only okay with that, but totally and completely powerful.

Course correcting all at once may be too much for you. It can cause your head to spin. It can be overwhelming to think about, resulting in remaining paralyzed because you are frozen with fear of backlash. This is not unreasonable at all. You've been conditioned to feel that way from the beginning. Many times, when you've been dealing with a narcissist, you've been dealing with what I call "narcissist erasure." This is where the narcissist has invalidated you, your feelings, and your needs so many times that walking forward and going on the offensive right away is too fast of a move right out of the gate.

Three Steps to Shifting the Dynamic of Power

When you are creating your Action Plan, it might be easier for you to think of it in terms of three steps.

Step 1: Don't Run. This is where you stop the conditioning, stop yourself from retreating and stop walking backwards. This is where you will draw boundaries and start to do some things that might feel uncomfortable. Small changes, small shifts, but very, very important.

Step 2: Make a U-Turn. This is where you turn around. This is where you will create a plan for negotiating that will start to shift the dynamic of power and create your leverage. Much more about how to create leverage in Chapter 6.

Step 3: Break Free. You will start walking forward. This is where you will actually present your offers and start speaking. I also go over how to powerfully present your offers in Chapter 8.

It is throughout this period that you are reclaiming your sense of self and your power, slowly but surely, knowing that somewhere inside, you never left.

Your Action Plan must have thought everything through, from the beginning of the process to the end, and you will reassess it as you move through it, making sure that the actions and the plan are still adhering to your Vision Statements and getting you to the outcome(s) you want to achieve. You want to be able to get there as quickly and as efficiently as possible, but also with the understanding that you will have to have patience. Your Action Plan must be narcissist-proof. If there is a weak spot, you can bet the narcissist will find it. It is a bit of a long game. It will not happen overnight.

The other thing you will have to have is fortitude. You want to be sure you never give in and never give up, and the narcissist will give you lots of reasons to want to. Remember they are like a two-year-old having a tantrum. If Mom and Dad haven't given in yet, then they just cry louder and longer. They think, *If I am annoying enough, they'll have to give in.* That's exactly what's going on with the narcissist.

I will let you in on another little secret: *they are the absolute worst right before they are ready to give up.*

So now let's start creating your Action Plan.

Step 1: Don't Run

This first step is to stop yourself from retreating. This step is designed to start protecting you in the relationship with the narcissist. Whether the relationship is business or personal, a shift is going to have to be made. The narcissist has been conditioning you from the beginning, and certain expectations have grown out of that relationship on the narcissist's part. They expect you to respond or behave in a certain manner, and if you don't, then they will respond or act accordingly. Thus, when you make shifts in the relationship, they may start acting like that toddler having a tantrum, depending upon the relationship, and depending upon how much they think it will trigger you.

The first thing you can do to stop the retreat is to create boundaries. Boundaries will be tremendously important for you, because this is the only way that you are going to start letting the narcissist know that you are shifting. It also allows you room to start to breathe and begin to heal, especially if you've been in any kind of a longer-term relationship with the narcissist. There are several ways to start creating boundaries that will also help to protect you in your negotiations as well as help you to create leverage going forward.

One of those ways to start forming boundaries is to find one form of communication. I recommend that form of communication to be in email if possible. I prefer email to text, because I think in terms of what would be optimal trial exhibits. Email has a time and date stamp and is less likely to be manipulated, and you have a record of the entire conversation. If you have children, and you are dealing with custody issues, then court-approved communication apps also work well.

The next part of your Action Plan is to start documenting everything properly. This will be a critical part of the foundation of creating your invincible leverage.

How to Create Fierce Documentation Like a Boss

Documentation is your golden ticket to the promised land. This is the key to everything. It is from your fierce documentation that you will eventually create that "magic bullet" leverage. That leverage will ultimately be what you use to ethically manipulate the manipulator into working with you in a normal, reasonable-person way.

Whether it is capturing video evidence, documenting emails, text threads, or lack of promised correspondence, or gathering proof of assets, documentation will become your protection against the narcissist in your life. Keeping track of everything will help to catch the narcissist amid their lies and schemes and provide real evidence against them.

The documentation is your protection, and the leverage is your ammo. You need both to safely enter your negotiation with a narcissist. As we walk through the steps of gathering your documentation and creating leverage, I'll help you to get right where most people go wrong. It's all about getting the narcissist to settle on *your* terms, in a way that makes them believe they are doing things on *their* terms.

What does documentation even mean? Documentation is a collection of information, facts, data, records, or potential information from people that can be used down the road. If you have a court case, it could be used for that. If your negotiation is for business, it may just end up being good leverage.

Why do you need fierce documentation? Because this is where the gold lies. This is where you spin straw into gold. This is your holy grail. Obviously, you present it only when you've decided, according to your Strategy and tactical plan, that it is best to present it. But this is where the rubber will hit the road. If you don't want to spend hundreds of thousands of dollars and years and years getting absolutely nowhere, this is how you do it. You will be taking your documentation and turning it into leverage.

While most people think that leverage is that one smoking gun, that one thing that's going to change everything, most of the time, the real leverage comes out of your documentation. The key is going to be in seeing the patterns or the information that emerge from your documentation.

For example, you can demonstrate that of the thirty times someone was supposed to make a monthly payment to you, they only paid it on time 38 percent of the time. Or that someone lied or made inconsistent statements in their emails and text messages forty-four times in six months. This is how you can potentially expose a narcissist.

It's when you analyze the data that you collect that you start to see where you can create summaries of the information, then attach the raw data as supporting documentation to the summaries. This is what becomes tremendous and bulletproof leverage. Here is where, when you compile all this information and then present it at the perfect time to the narcissist, they will be running scared out of their minds. They won't believe that you kept track of everything and then put it into an organized presentable form.

What should you be keeping track of?

Notes

The first way you can document is simply through your own notes. It doesn't have to be fancy or difficult. Just literally whip out your phone and keep a journal of everything that happens that seems like it may matter down the road. Remember that the absence of something happening might matter too. What I mean by that is that if someone is supposed to do a task at work every day and then doesn't do that task, then you can keep track of that in a calendar, and that calendar can then become your documentation. I have literally won entire trials on people's documentation, as long as it was kept regularly and simultaneously with the events occurring (or not occurring).

A very important thing to remember here is that when you are keeping track of these daily activities, you want to stick to the facts. Write down things that happened or didn't happen, but do not add any emotions, judgments, or feelings. You are literally just detailing activities in this sort of log.

Correspondence

Texts, emails, and other correspondence are another form of documentation. I absolutely love what this can turn into, but you do have to do some work. You will want to have some sort of system for keeping track of the correspondence itself. For example, if you have a lawyer and you are embroiled in some sort of litigation, you will probably be getting copies of letters between your lawyer and the other side's lawyer on a regular basis, so set up some sort of filing system right away to keep it all organized. If you don't have any sort of litigation going, then the kind of correspondence you will want to keep is just anything that seems pertinent or important that is related to your issues.

The Alchemist and *Rumpelstiltskin* are two stories I love, because of the idea of being able to take something of little value and be able to spin it into gold. That is the principle behind the secret of what I am about to share with you here. We know that all narcissists lie, right? Constantly. They can't help themselves. What they don't count on is that anyone will ever take the time to put together a summary of their lies and inconsistent statements. Remember that credibility is *always* relevant. Thus, you can literally take a text message from one month and match it up with a text or email from another month, put it together in a summary, place it together in a tab in a binder, and there is Tab 1 of Summary of Lies and Inconsistent Statements. Then do the same thing for Tab 2 and keep going. This now can even be an exhibit for a mediation or a trial if you need it to be. The more you have, the more impactful that piece of leverage becomes. Beautiful, right?!

Conversations

This can be with the other person or with others, where the conversation may be one that you might want to remember. Don't try to rely on your memory. You can't! Keep a journal of conversations that you believe may contain pertinent dates, times, or context or use a notes app on your phone. You can also "follow up" with confirmation correspondence, if necessary, with the other person. ("This is to confirm our conversation of today where we discussed…")

Again, remember to be factual. Do not add any emotions, judgments, or feelings. Keep any curse words out too. If you end up making copies of your journals to attach to summaries, you want to make sure that you end up being the one who the judge sees as the "good" one. Underneath the black robe, the judges are people with biases, they make decisions about who to believe and whose word they can trust, and you never know what is going to sway them. Don't give them any reason to think that it can't be you.

Photographs, Videos, and Audio Recordings

Photographs, especially those that you have taken yourself, can be a fabulous form of leverage. I say those you have taken yourself, because if by chance you end up having to testify in court, then those you have taken yourself will be the ones that will be the most easily admissible. Think about the photographs that will best document, further your Strategy, and create the leverage you need. Are they work photographs, leisure, vacation? What activities or people should be documented?

I also wanted to note video and audio recordings. While video and audio recordings may not often be played in court, they can still sometimes be great leverage, by the way. They can often still be played for custody evaluators or for other people by whom the narcissist may not want the video to be seen, so while many people do know that video and audio recordings aren't admissible, they can still be very good leverage, so definitely keep those if you have them.

I do also want to note that if you are having depositions done in a litigation case, definitely spend the few extra dollars to have it videotaped if you can afford it. Narcissists, especially grandiose and malignant types tend to act up in regular depositions, because they know that everything is being typed down. In other words, when the deposition transcript then comes out, the reader can only see Q, then the question, A, then the answer; the judge, or anyone else reading it, can't see if the person made faces or acted inappropriately, unless someone states on the record that they did. Many times, the narcissist will take the opportunity to act inappropriately or try to intimidate the other side if they can get away with it. Therefore, I advise you to get a videotaped deposition. It is a little bit more money, but it puts controls on the other side and forces them to behave a bit better, or it captures their bad behavior if they act up.

Potential Witnesses

Potential witnesses are another form of documentation, whether they know they are or not. These are people who you may or may not end up calling if there is potential litigation. But these can be a fantastic form of ethically manipulating the manipulators, especially when the new forms of supply have made their appearances. The narcissists definitely do not want to be exposed in front of the new form of supply, so will scramble to make sure the situation is secure.

Here's how this situation may play out. You go to the negotiation. You are prepared to resolve your situation. You have a complete agreement ready for the other side to sign. If there is an open case, then you can have subpoenas for depositions and/or witness lists ready to be filed. These will contain the names of people whom you know the narcissist definitely does not want you to speak to. Let them know that the choice is theirs. That they can sign the agreement, or they can choose not to sign, but if they choose not to sign, then you will be having your lawyer speak to the people in these subpoenas or on these lists. They will often not choose the second option because of that sparkly Diamond Level Supply that must be protected at all costs.

Research

Research can also be a form of documentation. This can include legal research, google research, data, interviews, facts, figures, and any supporting documentation that you have to back up your research.

What will you want to be researching yourself? Remember, in dealing with narcissists, they derive all their value from external sources, so if you want to resolve your issues with a narcissist, you need to figure out early on what your goals are, what value you have to give in this negotiation, and what value you want to be able to get.

This means that you will want to start with your side of the equation. What areas will you need to look at? While you are doing your own research, take the time to step back and think about the situation objectively. Decide if you are making assumptions that may or may not be correct. Be open to possibilities that are different from your initial assumptions. Dig as deeply as you can.

By gathering your research, you are starting the process of formulating your arguments as to why your position is the stronger one. You will want the other side to consider your position, and the more cold, hard facts you have to support your side, the better chance you have at prevailing and getting what you want.

Now remember: do not, and I repeat do *not*, tell your narcissist about any of your findings as you are coming to them. Remember you always want to use the element of surprise with narcissists.

Next, research the other side. This is the part where you anticipate what the narcissist is going to do and say and be two steps ahead of them.

Another part of this step, which is less obvious, is that you must do the other person's research. This means finding all the data, facts, figures, and information that the other person would dig up if he or she were doing the same sort of thorough research that you will be doing. Stand in the narcissist's shoes. Stand in the shoes of their lawyer.

Now, your circumstances may be such that you may already know the narcissist pretty well and how they think. Remember that whatever position you take, they are going to say it's wrong, it's faulty, that you're going to lose, that you're full of crap. You'll have to wear your Wonder Woman bracelets and push out your Superman chest and just deflect, deflect, deflect as you keep moving forward. But as you do that, also understand what they're thinking so you can anticipate what they will argue.

Social Media

Social media has become a very important source of leverage. Instagram, Facebook, Twitter, LinkedIn, and YouTube posts can give lots of information. By looking at what they are posting, you can often find out if there are, ahem, let's call them *discrepancies* in what the other side has been asserting. For example, I was representing a wife against a husband who was crying poor, even though he had made millions during the marriage. (Sidenote: all people who work for themselves who might have to pay alimony feign poverty during divorce; we call it SIDS—Sudden Income Deficiency Syndrome—but I digress....) But then his secretary girlfriend posted pictures of them on a yacht in Fiji on vacation, with her glass of champagne and her caption about how great life was. Busted! These are the sorts of ways that social media can help create leverage.

Finances

Financial documents are another great source of documentation. Depending upon whether this is a business situation or a personal situation, this could be QuickBooks, general ledgers, bank statements, credit card statements, income tax information, assets and liabilities information, property valuations, appraisals...the list really is endless. Sometimes people give this information to you as a matter of course, sometimes you have to subpoena it to force them to give it to you, but however you get it, you can then go through it carefully to look for opportunities to create leverage.

Again, you are looking for discrepancies. Have they lied? Are there inconsistencies? Is there something that can expose them? Is there something they wouldn't want another supply source to know? Always be thinking about your documentation strategically and through the lens of Diamond Level Supply and Coal Level Supply.

Agreements

Agreements can be another form of documentation that can be used as leverage. These can be formal or informal, oral or written, or complete or incomplete. You can send a text to say "Hey we just talked, and this is what we agreed to…" or there could be a full agreement written by lawyers that is notarized and dated. Whatever the form of the agreement, it can eventually potentially be used as leverage against the other side, depending upon the situation or what they are asserting or not asserting.

Timelines

I absolutely *love* timelines. I have used timelines to keep track of documentation myself. By using timelines, I can even shed light on lies by a spouse. For example, I realized that an opposing client was lying about when something happened, because I had the timeline and saw that it couldn't have happened when she said.

You are starting to build the foundation here of your Action Plan and stopping the retreat. I do recommend that you find a way to start organizing your documentation in a way that lets you keep track of it all and in a way that works for you.

In my SLAY program I show you how to organize your documentation, but if you would like a copy of my handy dandy Documentation-at-a-Glance chart for free, go to www.slay-thebully.com/resources and grab yours. Remember that this is literally the foundation for creating the magic bullet leverage.

Want to know what *really* makes the narcissist tick? What is the narcissist's true Achilles heel? That, my friends, is what we will be covering next in Chapter 6, on how to create invincible Leverage.

What Can You Do Now to Start SLAYing?

1. Let's create your Vision Statements. (Use a separate sheet of paper)
   - First, brainstorm everything that is most important to you.
   - Second, write out each outcome you want and if appropriate, when you want to achieve each outcome by.
   - Third, figure out your "why" for each statement.

2. Let's start creating your Action Plan
   - If you are thinking about making a change in the relationship with the narcissist, what do you have to do immediately to start protecting yourself?
   - What boundaries will you start to put in place?
   - Take a look at the forms of documentation I describe above. What kinds will you need to start keeping track of in order to start creating your leverage?

Mantra for Today:

I am making the decision to create a powerful Vision.
(Or write one of your own that speaks to you....)

CHAPTER 6

L: LEVERAGE, A.K.A. THE MAGIC BULLET

"Every battle is won before it is fought."
SUN TZU

It was the Stepford life that was all a bit too Stepford-y.

He was a CEO of a Fortune 20 company.

She was a smiling and adoring housewife.

He was powerful and charming.

She was demure and attractive.

She seemed to be the *perfect* wife.

They seemed to have the *perfect* life.

Just to give you a little more background on this couple, who we will call Mr. and Mrs. CEO, they met and fell in love while both were college students and had no money whatsoever. After college, Mrs. CEO landed a job in advertising, while Mr. CEO finished his MBA before starting his career. This meant Mrs. CEO was already soaring in her career when they got married a few years after college.

After the marriage, Mrs. CEO got pregnant right away. She then had a second baby right after that. She quit her career, he continued on with his, and yada, yada, yada, suddenly it was twenty-five years since she had worked at all.

For Mrs. CEO, while she had regrets, she poured herself into her family. Her children had attended great colleges, and they were grown and gone. While she didn't love how much time he had spent away, she looked forward to retirement with her husband.

Yes, Mr. CEO was controlling at home, but she was used to that. Yes, he called all the shots, didn't allow her to touch the finances, and could be emotionally abusive at times. But wasn't that how men were? She just wanted to live her life and not disturb the peace—especially at this stage in her life.

Except what she didn't know was that Mr. CEO had *dirty little secrets.*

Mr. CEO had a sex addiction. But this wasn't just any sex addiction. Nooo. That would not be exciting enough for this A-type personality. He didn't just enjoy porn in secret here and there, nor did a venture to a strip club from time to time satiate him. No, he had to have *escorts*, and over the years he had paid literally *thousands of women* for unprotected sex.

Mr. CEO's picture-perfect life was going, well, perfectly. He got to have his cake and eat it too.

That is until Mrs. CEO paid a visit to her OB-GYN, who informed her that the mysterious sores on her nether regions were in fact *genital herpes*!

"I'm sorry! Could you repeat that?" she said to the doctor. "That's impossible!"

This came to her as a shock, since *she* had never been unfaithful to *him.*

Once she recovered from this news, she filed for divorce.

I represented *Mrs.* CEO.

In this situation, Mr. CEO may have had all the power in the boardroom, and probably even at home. But, like magic, with leverage, everything shifted. He became the one with seemingly no power at all, because his wife knew his dirty little secret, and he definitely did *not* want anyone else to find out about his "hobby."

More often than not, it is not this glaring or this simple, but this example quickly demonstrates the power of leverage, and even more so, the power of narcissistic supply. Stay tuned and I will show you what I mean.

Leverage, which is the "L" in SLAY, is the information you hold to incentivize the other side. This leverage becomes your ammo against the narcissist. It's like an invisible magical bullet. This leverage is what the narcissist will never see coming.

That's because it is packaged in a way that is appealing to their own desires. But how do you get leverage?

First, you have to know what the other side wants. Consider what is driving them. What emotional investment do they have in the situation? What is incentivizing them? For people who aren't narcissistic, there are many different types of motivations. It could be money, time, or benefits. In a negotiation where two reasonable people are involved, the process can be solution-focused.

If there is a neutral third-party mediator or arbitrator, that person can listen to what both sides want and ensure that each side feels seen and heard. The neutral third party can then encourage each side to provide value to the other side so that the final resolution is one where both parties walk away feeling like they got something they wanted.

Narcissists, however, are very different. While narcissists are by far the most difficult personality on the planet, they are also the most *predictable* personality on the planet.

Remember what I told you in Chapter 2? Narcissists are driven by one thing and one thing only: narcissistic supply. Knowing this is the Key to the Kingdom. By understanding narcissistic supply and why they need it, you create your invincible leverage.

You must think outside the box here a bit.

Leverage could be who wants the settlement faster. This can be a motivator at times for narcissists, especially if they are dying to get on with their new forms of supply. It could also be that they are in a hurry to get a deal done before something is going to happen. There are all forms and types of leverage, and when you're dealing with a narcissist, you will want to get creative and make sure you're considering them all. But remember to always think of their motivation in terms of *narcissistic supply*.

As a reminder, supply is anything that feeds a narcissist's feeling of self-worth, but it's all layered on *externally*. They attempt to make themselves feel better internally by sucking as much from their outer world as they can, because that's the only way that they believe it's possible for them to be worthy. This is why they do whatever they can in a desperate attempt to "feed" that black hole, but it never gets filled.

Their sources of supply then become everything to them, and they see their sources not as people but rather as possessions. The supply sources can be analogized to the cans or jars of food people keep in their basements or cupboards to store for the winter. During the winter, they may not need those sources, but they know they are there. If you continue to serve any purpose whatsoever to the narcissist, they will want to store you, or keep you around, because they might want to use you later. If you don't, then you can be thrown out with the trash or put out with the garage sale items.

They will go after the next best source they can, while simultaneously trying to grasp onto the source they still have, all while testing to see if there are other sources out there that might be better. It's a constant balance of hunting and maintaining the current supply source.

Now, while this hunt and maintenance is going on, there is also this desperate attempt to make sure no one else knows that they are hunting or maintaining anything or anyone.

The worst thing for the narcissist would be for others to see the starving two-year-old child underneath. To remain covered, they use the "false self" I described in Chapter 3: the "pretend" version of themselves. This is how they become likable to different targets. They *become* what that target desires.

The problem is that the starving inner false self can never *truly* be fed. As the narcissist tries different types of supply and goes through different stages of narcissist abuse, the black hole that they are trying to fill remains feeling empty. (Think Oliver: "Please sir, I want some more.")

But, depending upon the severity of their narcissism, they are literally *addicted* to getting as much supply as possible at all times.

The Hierarchy of Narcissistic Supply

Most people who understand narcissism understand the concept of narcissistic supply.

What I have come to understand is totally different from what most people think about narcissists, and this is what completely changed everything for me.

Am I exaggerating? I think not. We are talking about narcissists here. Those who have made your life miserable and made you feel like you were going crazy, like something was innately wrong with you, completely disrespected, disregarded, unimportant, and like a broken person.

This is the revelation you've been waiting for.

As I discussed in Chapter 2, I've discovered that there is a hierarchy to narcissistic supply: Diamond Level Supply, which is always tied into how they look to others, and Coal Level Supply, in other words, the chosen few who are the narcissist's "targets." These are the people whom the narcissist decides to "possess." Yes, that's the word I deliberately chose for a reason. They view people as possessions. Possessions who are meant to serve their need for supply. Either these people will provide supply to them in the form of giving them some sort of value for value—meaning if the narcissist does something for them, they had damned well better be getting at least tenfold back in return—they are making the narcissist look good by being associated with them, or they serve some other purpose such as boosting the narcissist's ego or providing sex.

The other way that targets provide supply to narcissists is when the narcissist can whip out their dreaded Triple Ds—the Degrading, Debasing and Denigrating behavior. They save the Triple Ds for those whom I call the Double Vs—the Vulnerable Victims, or in other words, their targets. Narcissists get supply, meaning that they are attempting to feed that little beast inside themselves by making others feel small so they can try to feel bigger or look bigger. They actually enjoy manipulating you and intimidating you.

People think: *Narcissists just want to win!*

So, they give them everything thinking, *That'll do it! I can walk away! I'm free!*

But noooooooooooooooooo.

Pulled in. Sucked in. *Wait, what??*

I gave you everything!!!

Remember how Dr. Joe Vitale said he was willing to walk away in his divorce, and still his former wife made him miserable?

The myth that narcissists just want to win is dead wrong. Here's why.

"Winning" only considers one part of the narcissistic supply question: Diamond Level Supply. It totally forgets about Coal Level Supply.

It forgets that narcissists love to trigger you. They love to get under your skin.

And they sure as hell hate to give up any of their supply *willingly*.

Here's what's going on for non-narcissistic people: people who are reasonable also are constantly trying to see reason. Non-narcissistic people think narcissists want to save money or get money. Non-narcissistic people think narcissists want to win and look good by winning.

Non-narcissistic people don't realize that there's a whole secondary agenda going on at the same time, called Coal Level Supply. Narcissists probably don't even realize it themselves. Judges certainly aren't wise to it yet. Neither are lawyers, mediators, arbitrators, nor anyone else in the court systems who probably *should be*.

If you are negotiating contracts on a regular basis in a corporate setting, a sales setting, or any other setting, you definitely need to know this too. This is the side that is like the little kid that enjoys taking a pin and using it to prick an earthworm just to see it squirm for curiosity, for fun, for enjoyment, for amusement. They *don't want to see a resolution, because they are enjoying watching you squirm.*

This is why they move the goalposts in negotiations constantly. What do I mean by "move goalposts"? They give you an offer. You spend three days deciding if you even want the offer, because it isn't even very good. You talk it over with your friends and family. You go over the pros and cons. You decide that while it isn't what you even wanted, that at least it will be over, you won't have to spend any more on attorneys, and your sleepless night will be done. You can go on with your life. So, you go back to the narcissist and say that you'll take the deal. But guess what? That deal? It's no longer on the table!

Then they want to hold you to the parts that you agreed to do for them, but they don't want to have to be held accountable for the parts they were supposed to do, and the cherry on top of this nightmare ice cream sundae is that they blame the whole thing on you. It's your fault that the deal fell through, for whatever reason that they decided to manufacture that day. Let's see...here are a few of the types of reasons they might come up with: because you took too long to respond, because you didn't provide the documentation that you were supposed to provide, because you caused it to rain that day—well, you get the picture.

You are left so baffled and confused.

Winning? Yeah, that's nice—they definitely want that. But they also want to manipulate you, trigger you, make you squirm, and just generally make your life miserable.

You can't negotiate in a normal way with someone who wants to make your life miserable.

The normal rules of negotiation will not work. Will never work with narcissists. In fact, if you try to give a narcissist empathy, you're just feeding them supply. It's like blood in the water to a shark. Totally the wrong thing if not done tactically the right way.

So, you've gotta find a way to do a little something that I call ethically manipulating the manipulator.

How Do You Combat This Game?

You have to—no, let me rephrase that—you *must* have a Strategy which includes leverage. But not just any kind of leverage. My kind of leverage.

The key to leverage will be figuring out what source of supply is more important to them (usually Diamond Level Supply) than the supply that they get from making their target's life miserable.

Then you create a situation in your negotiations, through building the right leverage, so that you make the narcissist *feel* like their Diamond Level Supply *might* be exposed. In other words, you threaten a supply source that they are going to be willing to protect and defend, so that they then let go of that other supply source, which was jerking you around—the Coal Level Supply. Tactically, you hold back on actually exposing them, because if you do, then your leverage is gone. You have to make them feel like that Coal Level Supply just isn't worth the risk of losing their precious Diamond Level Supply.

How does this look in real life? Let's go back to Mr. and Mrs. CEO. He had all the power in the marriage, and he thought he had all the power in the divorce. Classic narcissist. He was doing all the things classic narcissists do.

Until she found out some things he had been doing in his private life that, if they were made public, could ruin him. She may have suggested during the course of negotiations that perhaps people might find out said things—in other words, should he fail to see reason, we would file a civil action for assault and battery and demand a jury trial, which meant we would then be allowed to depose many people in his world. Clearly, he didn't want the whole world knowing about his "hobbies," so he decided to come to an agreement in private. Suddenly, he was reminded of his vulnerability, namely that his cherished Diamond Level Supply might be exposed, so he decided to let go of the Coal Level Supply, the supply he was getting from jerking her around, and we were able to settle the case. In other words, she used my SLAY Method®. Get it?

The narcissist will do literally anything to make sure to protect that Diamond Level Supply. In reality, they want to keep all forms of supply because they are supply whores. They are like vultures picking the meat off the bones of the carcasses, checking to see if there's anything left, even going back to see if there's anything they've missed. But at the end of the day, like Meryl Streep in the movie *Sophie's Choice*, if they are forced, they will give up the Coal Level Supply to protect the Diamond Level Supply.

Many people falsely believe that you can start off nice and give up all sorts of things at the beginning, and that somehow you can garner some favor with the narcissist down the road in the negotiations. This is a huge myth. They will not see that you did anything for them. They will simply take what you gave them, without acknowledgement, with full entitlement, as if it were owed to them, and keep going.

How Do You Get Leverage?

Obviously, it is everyone's dream to have the kind of "smoking gun" leverage like Mrs. CEO had. But in most instances, you will not have leverage like that. Most of the time, you will have to create it. There are a number of ways to create leverage, but one of the most effective ways is through documentation, which is what we started to create in Chapter 5.

Once you create your documentation, then you start to see patterns emerge. You'll start to be able to build summaries such as a Summary of Lies and Inconsistent Statements, a Summary of Late Payments, or a Summary of Times They Were Late Picking Up the Child. The biggest thing to remember here is not to think that you can skip over this step.

By writing it all out, doing the timeline, and looking over all your documentation, you will get these major aha moments and see major patterns. Then you will need to think to yourself: *What form of the Diamond Level Supply matters the most to the narcissist that I am dealing with?* Then build your leverage in terms of that.

If you want the narcissist to leave you alone forever, then *that* is how you have to think strategically.

They will *never* leave you alone if they can continue to have their cake and eat it too, meaning as long as they can have their Diamond Level Supply and their Coal Level Supply too.

If they are still coming around you, it's because they are still getting some sort of supply by jerking you around. Period. You haven't figured out the formula yet.

This formula always works.

But you must build it around them almost like you are building an invisible fence that will only be revealed at the last second.

Then *switched on*! Like a light that gets turned on!

They realize it's there! That fence. You have them pinned in with nowhere to go except where you want them. Squeezed. They have no choice but to come to a peaceful agreement with you.

That reveal? That's you springing that leverage on them.

Step 2: Make a U Turn

Remember in Chapter 5, how I talked about a three-step process of righting the ship or turning it all the way around, 180 degrees, so that you're now going on the offensive?

First, Step 1: Don't Run. Stop the conditioning here.

Second, Step 2: Make a U-Turn. This is when you pivot, and this is how you do that—by creating invincible leverage. This is when you start to shift the dynamics of power.

Next, you'll spring your leverage on the other side. That's you going on the offensive. That will be "Step 3: Break Free"—you will start walking forward.

When Should You Spring Your Leverage on the Other Side? (Timing Is Everything)

The next key element, now that you have identified your leverage, is to not give it away too early in the game. You'll want to be sure you are saving your leverage for when you are going to need it. I once had a client who made this fatal mistake. It was a highly contested, overly litigated family law matter (overly litigated because the parties couldn't stop themselves from continuing the battle—pretty sure now, looking back, that they were both narcissists, but I digress). The soon-to-be-ex-husband, who was my client, was still living in the marital residence, and the future-former-wife had moved out. However, when she moved out, she left her old cell phone in the home.

He plugged in the phone, and there were all sorts of incriminating texts and emails. These were excellent trial exhibits for our case. He emailed us all of these very useful texts and emails, then that night, when he couldn't sleep, he started drinking wine and stewing on these texts and emails, and he sent all of them over to her with his choice words.

Translation: he took his great leverage and handed it right on over to the other side. This gave her the opportunity to be prepared, to spin them, to have an explanation, and basically to take all the wind from the sails of what could have been fantastic leverage.

The key in all of this is to have a clear idea of what you want, then to build a strategy for how to get there and employ the right tactics along the way. It is imperative to have a true understanding of what you do want out of the resolution and what you can live without as you negotiate. So many people skip over this step or don't put enough thought into this.

My favorite time to present leverage, which I alluded to earlier, is at the negotiation itself. It could be at a mediation, arbitration, or even something less formal. But the optimum situation is one in which the narcissist *thinks* you are going to expose them, make them look bad, and/or turn the tables on them, and thus they will then jump at the chance to start playing nicely in the sandbox with you for a change. This means that what you will be doing with everything is holding it super close to the vest until everything is ready to present.

If you are negotiating in the context of a lawsuit, in the best-case scenario, you will want to have that full formal written agreement prepared, which lays out exactly what you want. You might even want to have a couple of versions prepared. Also, have it near you, so you can modify it quickly and easily. Use Google Docs, for example, and have your laptop and a printer close at hand. Then you will present all your leverage at the same time and give them the choice to sign the agreement, or else you will move forward with your plan.

They have to feel like you've sprung an invisible trap on them, and there is no other way to go. They can't wriggle out of this. They can't move the goalposts. This is when you'll see one of two things happen: the charm gets turned on ("Oh come on, we can do this," "We don't need all of this"), or narcissistic rage will come flying out ("You're a scumbag," "You're horrible," "You have no conscience," and so forth). This is where you will have to control your emotions. Don't be triggered. Don't blink. You've spent lots of time leading up to this moment.

But we are getting ahead of ourselves. There's a lot more you'll have to do before you get to that. I will get more into how to powerfully present your offer in Chapter 8.

A Quick Word for Those Who Are Feeling a Bit Cringe-y

For some people, particularly women, or others who think leverage means "game-playing," this may be a difficult topic. Many people will say to me that they don't want to fight, that they don't want to appear greedy, or just that they simply don't want to play games. They believe they can just talk things through. This is absolutely the case with rational, reasonable people, but not with narcissists.

Remember that a narcissist at his or her core is a damaged personality, who, underneath it all, has the worst case of self-loathing and the lowest self-esteem. For that personality type, the *only* thing that brings value is the external. Thus, there is only one way that you will get where you want. You'll have to figure out a way to turn their pain points or arguments against them, or close in the walls around them, so that they have no other choice but to finally give in. You never know when that point will be for a narcissist. Some of the worst ones won't give in, no matter what, until their backs are against that proverbial wall.

I had a case one time where I was representing the husband. It was a fourteen-year marriage, and the wife, while she hadn't worked regularly while the kids were little, had an MBA and CPA and was working while the case was pending. She insisted on asking for gobs of alimony—more than my client earned! She was a malignant narcissist, one who had called the police claiming false allegations of domestic abuse, so we had no choice but to go to trial. That day, the judge decided to turn the day into a glorified mediation. He went on to tell her in open court that he would never order a penny of alimony to her and that she should settle the case.

Frustratingly, he didn't then order anything at all, but instead asked the parties to continue settlement discussions and then set a date for a month later to come back for either a trial, if they hadn't settled, or to let him know what the settlement was. What do you think happened? Right-o! She didn't settle! She continued to insist that my client was hiding income and that she was entitled to alimony.

But then guess what happened? She settled right before she walked back through the doors on the day they had been ordered to go back. Yep. She didn't want to face that judge again! (Because if she had to face the judge, her Diamond Level Supply would have potentially been exposed. She would have lost the respect of the judge. She could have lost the case publicly. Everyone in her world would have found out.) But she also didn't want to pass up the opportunity to make my client's life miserable all the way up until the very last second.

See how she protected her Diamond Level Supply by letting go of her Coal Level Supply? But she waited until the very last possible millisecond to do it. She squeezed every ounce out of both forms of supply for as long as she possibly could. In the end, though, the Diamond Level Supply won out—as it always does.

Create Your First Offer

Before you walk into the room, you want to have your first offer ready to go. This will be in the range of your best-case scenario. Then decide ahead of time what you're going to be willing to give up. This helps you control the process. Make sure you are asking for much more than what you are going to be willing to settle for.

Remember that people must sort of be "beaten up" by the negotiation process before they'll come to a resolution sometimes. There are so many times that I have seen people end up at the exact same point as if one party had offered to resolve the matter at the outset. Oftentimes, until they've been tossed about in the negotiation boat and gotten seasick a few times, they still have grandiose ideas about how much they are going to get or what they think is a "fair" settlement.

By having your first offer ready and then deciding ahead of time what you're going to be willing to part with or, put another way, what the minimum is that you can live with, you will feel more in control of the process as it starts to unfold.

Now, once you have your first offer in mind, definitely don't even hint at what it is going to be before you are totally ready to present it along with your leverage and everything else. In fact, if you're feeling bold, you might want to try to throw them off the scent. In other words, act like there is something you really want, which you actually don't care about. Because if there's a hint in the air of what you might want, then that will be the thing that they make it their mission to be sure you don't get.

Yep. Ethically manipulating the manipulator.

Figuring Out What to Ask For

People who go into a negotiation having done their research feel a sense of confidence and empowerment because they have the market information to support their position. Thus, depending upon what it is that you are negotiating for, have an understanding of whether or not you will need to move from your position or what they will have to do to move from theirs.

It's also important to go into a negotiation with an idea of what you're willing to accept if your first offer doesn't fly. If you decide before the negotiation what you're willing to accept (and what you're *not* willing to accept), you're less likely to make a rash decision on the fly or get talked into something and regret it later.

When Should the Negotiations Happen?

This is a crucial thing to consider with anybody, but as with everything else with a narcissist, it's magnified. It's basically like you're coaxing a little squirrel to come over and get an acorn out of your hands, any big, sudden movements can and will set them off, and no matter how hard you try to make them feel better or assuage their ego, they still perceive you as against them, simply because you aren't *for* them.

They are going to try to twist anything and everything. This means that for sure you do *not* want to negotiate with a narcissist in a situation where they will become more upset or agitated.

If, by the way, during the negotiations, they are making it seem like everything can be harmonious again, it's more than likely a ploy to get control back over you. (Remember everything they do is some form of manipulation.) Or it could just be that they are nursing their narcissistic injury, so they don't want you to leave, but either way, you can try to spin it and use it to your advantage. Let them think that you are considering it.

If they want you to believe that they have sincerely changed, then simply call their bluff and ask them to just enter into a written agreement right away. Create an agreement that controls the parameters going forward and protects you. They probably won't sign it, and then you will have "snuffed out the bluff," as I like to say. Either way, it works to your advantage.

But going back to the timing, there are really two times when the timing is going to be important here. The first is when you actually ask for the meeting. The second is the time and place of the meeting itself. For both, you will want to be sure that the other person is in a place to hear what you are saying.

For the first part, where you are simply asking for the meeting, the timing is a bit less critical. You can perhaps email the person so that they can take a look at the email whenever they have the time to do so. The way you ask for the meeting will also be important. Leave off any tone of accusation, anger, or judgment. A simple request without emotion or fighting words will be perfect.

If you both have lawyers, the lawyers can set up a meeting with the four of you, or you can also hire a neutral mediator. I highly recommend hiring a good, strong mediator if you have a lawsuit of any kind going, and you will likely want to be in different rooms. You don't know what can set off the narcissist or how the narcissist can set you off, and you want to get to a resolution.

The mediator can sort of "cleanse" messages between the two of you and keep everything on track regarding the actual issues at hand. This means that the mediator can present the offers in a way that is optimal so that you will each hear them.

Your negotiation conversation is also important. Plan it correctly. Make sure the person with whom you need to speak is open to setting the meeting when you approach them about having a meeting initially, then be sure that when it is scheduled, it is scheduled for a time and place when and where you both will feel heard.

For both sides to feel like they matter, both sides will want to be able to speak and feel valued, so timing the conversation properly will be an important step toward winning what you want.

With a narcissist, you often only get a chance, or maybe two at the most, before they just fly off and decide they want the judge to decide or that they don't care if you never get what you want.

If it's not a litigation matter, then you will still only get one or two bites at the apple at the most with a narcissist before they fly off and just decide that they are done. Narcissists do not have a lot of patience with the negotiation process. Plus, they trust absolutely no one. They don't resolve issues, even when they should, even if it's in their own best interests. Remember you're not dealing with a rational person here.

Remember never to apply rational thinking to their irrational behavior. You'll never come to a logical conclusion.

Where Should the Negotiations Take Place?

Again, I want to reiterate that you don't want to be alone with the narcissist, so you want to stay clear of that. A lot of psychological studies have been done on whether you should go to their turf, use your turf, or go to a neutral one. Of course, there is a lot of evidence that your turf is advantageous to you. You've heard of the "home field advantage." However, when you're dealing with a narcissist, having them come to your office, your lawyer's office, or some other place that is going to set them off may not be a good idea.

This is an area where you might want to give them a couple of choices. Make sure you're fine with any of the options they choose, but give them the illusion that you are giving them control. Whenever you can give them options and not *tell* them what to do, you're more likely to get buy-in from them.

The Actual Day of Negotiation

The day of the actual negotiation will be a stressful one, but remember that 99 percent of a negotiation is won before you even walk into the room.

You will have done a lot of the work before you even walk into the room. Getting the narcissist to agree to anything in mediation or a negotiation is going to be tricky but not impossible, and you will be ready.

You will have to control your emotions. Don't be triggered—and don't blink. You've spent lots of time leading up to this moment.

You'll know exactly what to expect, and you will be *ready*. Because next, in Chapter 7, we move on to the next letter in SLAY—the A: Anticipating What They Are Going to Do and Being Two Steps Ahead of Them.

What Can You Do Now to Start SLAYing?

1. Let's create your Leverage and Offers. (Use a separate sheet of paper.)
    - What is most important to the narcissist in your life, as far as how they look to the world, or put another way, what is their "Diamond Level Supply"?
    - What is their "Coal Level Supply"?
    - What will be your best leverage?
    - What will be your first offer?
2. When and where should your negotiations take place?
    - When do you think your negotiations should take place?
    - Where do you think your negotiations should take place?

Mantra for Today:

I am excited about creating my new future.
(Or write one of your own that speaks to you….)

CHAPTER 7

A: ANTICIPATE WHAT THE NARCISSISTS ARE GOING TO DO, AND BE TWO STEPS AHEAD OF THEM

"Pay no mind to those who talk behind your back. It simply means that you're two steps ahead."

QUOTE OFTEN ATTRIBUTED TO TUPAC SHAKUR

"It sounds like you're dealing with a covert narcissist."

My friend, a psychologist, said these words to me over lunch. I didn't believe him at first, yet those are very words that have set my life on a whole new trajectory. I was stunned. I thought a narcissist was someone who was male, misogynistic, loud, openly arrogant, and boastful. Not an older woman who appeared to the rest of the world as kind.

"Nooo," I pushed back, though I was unsure of myself. "I mean, she's very insecure for sure, but I wouldn't say she's a narcissist!"

My friend insisted with full certainty. "Oh, she's one hundred percent a covert passive-aggressive narcissist," he said. He then suggested some books for me to read. I wasn't totally convinced, but I bought one book anyway.

I will never forget reading that first book on covert narcissism. It was *The Covert Passive Aggressive Narcissist* by Debbie Mirza, and I was blown away at how much it described not only the person I had been dealing with, but also a family member my husband and I had been dealing with.

Once I dove into not just that book, but many, many others, I started to recognize each type of narcissist—covert, grandiose, and malignant—and I started to recognize that once they are in litigation or negotiation, they are more prone to certain types of behaviors. Aha, grasshopper! This is when the rubber really hit the road for me.

When you start to recognize these patterns, you can discover not only that you are dealing with a narcissist, but what kind, and you can actually predict how they will behave and how to be two steps ahead of them.

Here are some examples:

Covert narcissists are more likely to:

> *Line up flying monkeys, but sometimes, under the guise of "caring" or "how sad it all is," weave in partial truths or paint themselves as the victim and you as their aggressor.*
>
> *Use passive-aggressive moves.*
>
> *Remain nice on the surface as long as possible.*
>
> *Do things underhandedly if they think they can get away with them, always ensuring plausible deniability if possible.*

Set themselves up to look like the victim.

Grandiose narcissists are more likely to:

File false pleadings.
Line up flying monkeys by feeding them outrageous lies.
Ignore court orders.
Pressure you to settle out of court.
Flagrantly manipulate evidence (texts/emails).
File meritless motions.

Malignant narcissists are more likely to:

Threaten to stalk you (or actually stalk you).

Lie about something that could ruin your career (for instance, accuse you of being a child molester or wife-beater in a pleading, when that has absolutely no basis in truth whatsoever).

Use violence or threats of violence.

Though narcissists become quite deft at disguising their motives and behaviors throughout their lives, once you know that you're dealing with a narcissist, while they are no less horrible and heinous to deal with, their patterns of behaviors are actually quite predictable. They are basically parasites or "Energy Vampires" who attach themselves to hosts and, once all the supply has been fully depleted from that source, move on to the next source of supply.

This is when it comes to the A in SLAY, which stands for Anticipating their behavior and staying two steps ahead of them. By being ahead of them:

You can predict their behavior, based upon their patterns.

You now have an understanding that because of their brain chemistry they will not behave or communicate as regular, reasonable people do, so you won't expect them to do so.

You understand that they will be actively trying to trigger you at all times, so you can engage tools to arm yourself against their attempts to unglue you, and you won't take the bait.

We've all heard the adage "Prepare for the worst and hope for the best." That wisdom especially applies when dealing with narcissists. Whether you want to negotiate your way out of a financial settlement, a business partnership, or a divorce, you never want to be surprised by the opposing side. Anticipating what the opposing side in the negotiation is going to do or is going to want will help you to carry out your Strategy, so you can use your Leverage in the most advantageous way.

While a narcissist can seem out of control in their actions compared to others, they aren't entirely unpredictable. Think back to the different types of narcissists we talked about in Chapter 1. By identifying the narcissist, you are trying to negotiate with (either the grandiose, the covert, or the malignant), you can use the knowledge of their tendencies against them and thus in your favor. You can actually predict every argument or move the other side can make to a reasonable degree of certainty before you approach your negotiation. To the extent that you can, you will also always want to have a back-up plan and always show up more prepared than the narcissist.

When you have prepared, you'll be able to maintain your composure during your negotiation, even when the narcissist is acting like the totally incorrigible person they are. In this chapter, I will teach you how to anticipate, as much as possible, every aspect of your negotiation with a narcissist, so that you will be ready to refute any argument or position and be able to communicate powerfully. This will allow you to stay in control of the negotiation process, set the terms, and maintain the power all along the way.

Step 3: Break Free

This is when you move on to Step 3 of Shifting the Dynamic of Power. Remember when we discussed the three steps to shifting the dynamic of power in Chapter 5? You have stopped the conditioning, which was "Step 1: Don't Run," you have pivoted, which was "Step 2: Make a U-Turn," and now you will start communicating powerfully and then move to "Step 3: Break Free." This is where you'll regain your liberty from the narcissist!

Communications with a Narcissist

We know that the narcissist wants to trigger you. They love nothing more than seeing you get emotional. They get off on that!

So, anticipate that this is what they are going to do, and then you'll be ready for it. Don't allow yourself to be triggered by it. Don't show them that what they are doing is bothering you, for a number of reasons. One reason, of course, is that you don't want to give them the supply.

But another reason is that they are very likely to use your response against you. Just picture your narcissist just after doing something to make you lose it, smugly pointing at you while commenting, "Oh, look! See: you're the emotional one! You're the crazy one!" Do *not* give them that satisfaction.

A third reason not to show them they are getting to you is they will never leave you alone if you don't. Remember as long as they are getting supply, they will keep coming around. (Think of a peanut butter jar—as long as there is some left to scrape at the bottom, they will come back for it.)

Stop Defending Yourself

When you get those long emails or texts, very often they are carefully curated to trigger you. They'll tell you you're terrible with finances, that you're a deadbeat dad, that you never did anything for the company, that they never loved you, or that you're an awful mother. Suddenly you want to defend every single point.

Here's what I say to that.

Stop defending yourself. It's a natural reaction. Believe me. I want to do it too, when I'm attacked. But if you defend yourself when you're attacked, you're agreeing there's an issue.

When you defend, you're giving the other person control, so whatever you do, please resist the temptation to defend yourself.

If you're not defending yourself, what will you do instead?

You will stand in your power.

I know: easier said than done, so I'm going to give you five strategies here for dealing directly with the narcissist. In Chapter 8, I will also give you strategies to manage your own fears and dread in dealing with the narcissist.

"Just the Facts"

This first strategy is called "Just the Facts." I named this one after the guy from the old television show *Dragnet*. Now, just for the record, he's before my time. He was a police sergeant who was known for asking people to stick to the facts, so the quote he's known for is: "Just the facts, Ma'am, just the facts."

Here, you will look at the situation as if you are completely disengaged. This is, without a doubt, ridiculously difficult. That's why the key is to keep all interactions as brief and unemotional as possible. You've hopefully started to draw your boundaries against the narcissist. In a perfect world, you are creating a new normal where you will no longer have this person as a part of your future. Alternatively, if this person is a part of your family, you are in a work situation, or this person must remain a part of your life on an ongoing basis, then drawing very strict boundaries will be a must.

Not being emotional when they are actively trying to provoke you is so hard. There is no doubt. I liken it to holding your breath. You can definitely do it for a few seconds if you need to. Then go scream into your pillow or cry in the shower. Just don't do it in front of them. Remember that old commercial that had the slogan "Never let them see you sweat"? Well, that goes quadruple-fold here! Narcissists will get supply from seeing you sweat. Do not give them that satisfaction! That means to remember that while you are interacting with the narcissist, whether it's in person, in writing, or on the telephone, provide "just the facts." "Just the facts."

What this means is that you can inform the other person of what is happening and provide data, but you do not add anything emotional, accusatory, or inflammatory. If it helps, pretend you are reporting the news.

Remember you don't owe them an explanation or a justification. You can respond, but don't react.

"The Middle Finger"

This next strategy I call "The Middle Finger." I learned this strategy from an attorney with whom I used to work. He was a formidable litigator. Super tough and very smart. Exactly the kind that you would want on your side if you were going up against the most malignant of narcissists, that's for sure.

As an attorney, you will definitely be pummeled with paper. By that I mean not only do you see lots and lots of false pleadings and motions being filed with the court, but you also get the correspondence coming through on a daily basis about what your client did or didn't do. Whether it's a business case or a family law case, there are always plenty of narcissists to go around, either as clients or as opposing clients, and they are constantly goading attorneys into sending accusatory letters or emails to the other side.

Then once that letter or email is received, the attorneys have to go back to their clients and find out what the "real story" is and try to craft some sort of response, knowing full well that it may end up as some sort of court exhibit down the road. Not only can that get to be expensive, but it can get into this back-and-forth that puts you into the position of being on the "defensive" and of giving away some information about your leverage or your side of the negotiations that you may not be interested in sharing just yet.

Thus, this attorney came up with this strategy, which I have affectionately termed "The Middle Finger," only because it will help you to remember it!

How this strategy works is very much like Just the Facts, but here you will be looking only at written correspondence. What you do is look through that long sea of crap that they sent you (whether it's text, email, Facebook, or direct message). You know that most of it was sent just to harass and purposely annoy you, but sometimes, just sometimes, there may be just one or two things in the correspondence that you do have to respond to.

I know you want to go point by point by point and respond. Do *not* do that.

If, for example, the only thing that you need to respond to is where and when to meet, here is how an alternative Middle Finger might look.

> *I am in receipt of your email.*
> *I deny your accusations.*
> *We can meet at 3 p.m. on Wednesday.*

You have said you received the email. You have denied everything all at once, and then you responded to the one and only thing that you needed to respond to. That's it. You don't need to go point by point.

Doesn't that feel so much more powerful? I have a lot more on how to communicate, including actual phrases and sample responses, in my SLAY program. But for now, understand that brevity is key. You can check out more out and grab a free "Crush My Negotiation Prep Worksheet" to get you started if you'd like at www.slaythebully.com/resources.

"Making a Plan, Stan"

In this strategy, which I call "Making a Plan, Stan," you will have an agenda, a plan, and/or a time limit when you go to speak to the narcissist about anything that you know will need to be negotiated or that will require any sort of discussion. You will definitely want to make sure that they know about the agenda in advance.

This sends a very clear message to the other side that you are limiting the conversation and helps you take control of the conversation as well. It will also help you during the conversation, because when it invariably goes beyond the scope of the topic, you can respectfully state that you are asking that the conversation stay within the scope of the agenda for that day's meeting. Similarly, if the conversation reaches the time limit, you can let the other person know that you have to excuse yourself. You can make up that you have a prior commitment or that you have to leave for any reason that you want, and you can even say you look forward to the next conversation.

This is you starting to take control. This is you starting to walk forward and not backward. I do want to throw in a few words of caution here, however. Depending upon their level of control and power over you historically, be careful about meeting with the narcissist alone. You may want witnesses. You may also want to consider hiring a strong neutral mediator to help.

"Fluff for Favor; Vomit Later"

With this strategy that I affectionately call "Fluff for Favor; Vomit Later," you will use the narcissist's love for Diamond Level Supply, but this time, you are going to use it to your advantage.

Once again, ethically manipulating the manipulator.

Here, you will do a little something called narcissistic "fluffing." This means that you will be fluffing up their egos like you would fluff up a pillow. Remember that one form of Diamond Level Supply is adulation or compliments. That is precisely what narcissistic fluffing is. It is stroking their ego a little bit or complimenting them—and if you can do this in front of other people that they highly respect, that's even better.

You will be doing this with purpose and very deliberately, and you will be doing this in exchange for getting something that you want in return. This is part of an overall plan. Please understand that I am not asking you to pander to this person or become a doormat. Quite the opposite. You will know what you are doing and why.

Here is an example: "Can you handle resolving the QuickBooks this month? You're so much more efficient at it than I am, and it would get done so much faster and more accurately than if I did it."

Make sure when you're engaging in this conversation that you are very careful not to have any sort of sarcastic tone. Narcissists hear tones like a dog hears whistles. By that I mean that even if you have no tone whatsoever, they hear tone. They're very easily slighted. Also, be sure not to include anything nice about yourself. What I mean by that is, using the above example, you would not say something like "I'm also good at QuickBooks, but I just don't have time, so I'm asking you, who I know is also a whiz." Even though you said they were good, they wouldn't be swayed, because you said something good about yourself in there. That would be enough to take away from the whole thing and maybe even torpedo the entire mission.

This strategy does two things at once. It satisfies their need for adulation and gives them Diamond Level Supply, and you get something that you want. You give them a little of what they want and get something you want in return.

You obviously use this sparingly and strategically.

And if you want to go shower or vomit later, that's okay.

This is why I call it "Fluff for favor; Vomit Later."

"COOL Words": When Negotiation Turns Red Hot in Intensity, How Do You Calm It Down?

Even before I knew I was dealing with narcissists, I would instinctively know somehow that if I let on to them that I was upset in some way, it would feed them.

During my years as an attorney, I have seen the full gamut of emotions during the actual negotiations, especially if they are in person. This is even more true if you have had a personal relationship with the narcissist. I have seen people punch holes into walls, yell, throw things, scream, and walk out. I have also seen people just completely shut down and stop talking altogether or full out sob on the floor. I have seen people so overtaken with fear that they were visibly trembling.

I can assure you that if you take the advice that I am giving you in this book, none of the above will pertain to you. Winning is a mentality. I actually used to say 80 percent of winning happened before you entered the room, but then I interviewed the legendary Bob Proctor, author of *You Were Born Rich*, who was featured in the movie *The Secret*, and he corrected me on *my own podcast* and said, "No, it's ninety-nine percent!" I agreed.

But a lot of that is staying calm and cool, not letting your emotions take over, and also having power mantras while you are in the room. So, I came up with the acronym "COOL Words." The word "COOL" is an acronym for how to keep your emotions in check, and the "Words" portion refers to your own power words that you will choose.

This advice is for during the actual negotiation, whether it is in person or even virtual.

1. *"C": Chill Out: Take a Break*

The "C" in "COOL Words" stands for "Chill Out." Take a break. You can just say, "Excuse me. I need a moment," and get up from the table. Go to the restroom and throw cold water on your face. Maybe take a deep breath. Take several deep breaths. Take a walk outside and get some fresh air. Just take a few minutes to yourself to calm down and let the intensity of the room also calm down. Because while you're taking a breath, the other person will be as well.

Another way to take a break may be to change up how you've been negotiating. For example, if you are using a mediator, maybe the mediator speaks just with you, with you and your lawyer, just with the other side, or just with their lawyers. Sometimes just making a shift in who's speaking with whom can help people to chill out and bring down the temperatures of everyone involved.

2. *"O": Observe Their Behavior Verbally to Them without Emotion or Judgment*

The first "O" in the "COOL Words" acronym is to observe their behavior verbally to them without emotion or judgment, so you might say something like "I can see that you're very upset," or "I can see that you are angry." Or you might even ask them what it is that's making them so angry in that moment. Get them to verbalize it.

You just want to take yourself out of it and observe their behavior to them or ask them to explain their behavior without judgment, without emotion, and without defensiveness. You don't get into it with them. You're simply observing.

3. *"O": Observe the Situation as If You Are a Bystander*

The second "O" in the "COOL Words" acronym is to observe the situation as if you are a bystander. This is where you are actually going to take yourself out of the situation, as if you are not part of it. You're just going to watch what's happening. Pretend like you're watching a two-year-old having a tantrum on the floor. They're screaming. They're yelling. You don't feel like you need to get down on the floor and scream and yell with them. You usually just watch them.

If it's helpful, start thinking of it as a game, like this is something that's happening in this moment but doesn't have to affect you.

Don't take anything they say or do personally, because the way people treat other people is always a reflection of the way they feel about themselves.

4. *"L": Let It Go by You*

Literally watch the words happening as if they're just flying by you. You can just step aside and watch them go. They're not touching you in any way.

It is as if you are saying to yourself, "Wow, that just whizzed by me!" When I was a kid, dodgeball was a big thing. I always really hated that game, because I felt like I was constantly under the gun with that ball. But I remember the times that I would actually dodge the ball, I would see it go whizzing by my head, it would hit the wall next to me, but it didn't hurt me at all. I would just observe it.

That's what I think of when I think of this. Just let the words whiz by you, hit the wall, and fall on the floor.

5. **"Words": Use Power Words as Your Mantra**

Okay, this is one of my super secrets, one that I actually used to use myself when I would go to trial. I would do this to help me focus and make sure that I had a powerful and winning mindset. This is seriously how I became one of the top lawyers. I pushed back against gripping fear by using this exact strategy.

What you will do here is write down certain "power" words, then keep them in front of you or, if you don't want people to see the words, then just use the first letter of the words. You will know what they mean. Put them where you can see them throughout the day.

Use these words to remind yourself of who you are. Your badass self. Your powerful self.

If it's a phone meeting or a Zoom meeting, it will be easier to have the words in front of you. If it's in person, maybe you just use an initial or a symbol. Nobody has to know what it means; it only matters if *you* know what it means. You can have power words that resonate with you such as:

Power
Strength
Leverage
Resilience
Confidence
Control

In the book *Think and Grow Rich*, Napoleon Hill talks about the power of autosuggestion, which is a way for you to reprogram your brain and your neuronal patterns. By having these power words to ground you, even when you are in that room and potentially going to be triggered, you will start to develop a habit of thinking of yourself as your badass self and staying in that mindset, no matter what happens.

So, remember "COOL Words" when the emotion heats up during the negotiation.

Anticipating Arguments and Being Ready to Smack Them Down

One of the most powerful tactics that I have found when presenting at a negotiation, whether it's a formal negotiation or not, is anticipating the arguments and then smacking them down before your opponent even has a chance to bring them up. What this would look like is saying something such as "I am anticipating that what you are going to argue is this: ______________. And here's my response to that: ______________. I'm also anticipating that you were going to have the position that ______________, and here is my response to that: ______________." And you go through every single one of their arguments and explain why their arguments don't hold water before they even have a chance to present them.

As an attorney, I have used this technique even at trial during my opening argument. Then, during my direct examination of my witnesses, I address the other side's arguments head on and shoot them down.

This is especially effective if you have a weakness on your side of the fence. Your instinct may be to hide your weaknesses.

But the converse is absolutely true. Bring your weaknesses right out, and then you control the narrative. If there's some fact that is going to come out that is not favorable to you—perhaps it was some behavior that you engaged in that they are planning to use against you—then don't sit aside hoping and praying it doesn't come out. The much stronger play is to say, "I am anticipating that you are going to bring up that I did this. You are correct. I did. However, here's all the reasons why that doesn't matter right now." My point is that *you* are one who decides how the game is going to be played this way, not them.

The idea here is that you take the wind right out of their sails and take them off balance. It weakens them. It's a power-play and gains an advantage over them psychologically, as well as in the negotiations themselves.

Other Secrets to Controlling Negotiations with the Narcissist

Be Overprepared

When you walk through the doors of the negotiation, or show up on that Zoom call, have your arguments, leverage, research, and everything ready to go. Whatever the holes are in your case or argument, the narcissist will sniff them out faster and more efficiently than a dog can sniff out a speck of steak on the floor. They are formidable at finding weaknesses in people, as they have made that their life's purpose.

Make sure you also have a first offer ready, and make sure that it is much more than you are ready to settle for.

Choke Point

Know what your "choke point" is ahead of time. This is what I also call your "walk away" point. The day of the actual negotiation can be emotional, so by knowing ahead of time what you are willing to settle for, you can alleviate some stress. Perform your risk analysis to know what your walk away point is. That way, if the negotiations reach that point, you will know it's time to stand up, shake hands, say, "Thank you very much," and walk out the door. No emotion.

How Are You Presenting Yourself?

What are you going to wear? There have been many studies done about how what you wear has a direct impact on your psyche. You will want to wear something that makes you feel like a million bucks. You want to feel confident and powerful, so choose something accordingly.

Colors have a direct impact on other people's perceptions of you psychologically. Many people think red is a good choice, but that can be an inflammatory color to wear. Yellow can be seen as weak. Black can be powerful but also could be divisive. Entire books have been written on this topic, but basically blue, purple, green, or white are all safe choices. I have a lot more on this in a YouTube video that you can find on my YouTube channel, at www.youtube.com/rebeccazungesq, and in my book *Negotiate Like You M.A.T.T.E.R.: The Surefire Method to Step Up and Win*, which you can find at www.slaythebully.com/resources if you're interested in learning more.

Develop a Rapport

Lastly, we come to developing a rapport. Listen, I know you can't stand the narcissist. I've totally been there, and as I said, it is not in my personality type to pander. I'd rather pull my own toenails off.

Seriously. But you want something from the narcissist, because if you didn't, why would you be bothering to negotiate with them? This is the same idea as "Fluff for Favor; Vomit Later." Suck it up, smile through the crap, shake their hand, say hello, and be cordial. (Please note: if you have any concerns for your safety, such as a history of domestic violence, disregard this advice.) Be the bigger person and show that they don't rattle you. Walk in with confidence and power. In Chapter 8, I will give you some exercises to help you with this too.

If you are in the same room, and they make an offer, you can repeat it, and you can acknowledge it. That helps them to feel like you heard them. Use your "COOL Words." Mirror their body language. That also helps them to feel more comfortable.

If you are mediating, then you might want to consider being in separate rooms and letting the mediator walk back and forth between the rooms. That will help keep the emotions down. The mediator, as I mentioned earlier, if they are good, can then sort of what I call "sanitize" offers, by presenting them in such a way that each side has a better chance of actually "hearing" them, so that there is a higher chance for resolution.

With narcissists, if you are in a litigation setting with them, then I absolutely recommend using a strong mediator, because you have a much higher chance of resolving your differences. Narcissists don't like looking bad or showing their "narc-y" side in front of people they respect like lawyers, judges, arbitrators, or mediators, so they are less likely to be total jackasses in mediation too. Not always—just usually.

Conclusion

The narcissist may be a formidable opponent, because they are relentless, unforgiving, ruthless, and cruel. But their weakness is that they are willing to lose the war to win battles. In other words, because they often lack the ability to regulate themselves emotionally and not act impulsively, and because their behavior is so predictable in the sense that they will almost always choose the low road instead of behaving nicely, it's actually somewhat simple to lay a trap for them. In fact, I'll bet that you can anticipate your narcissist's behavior with more accuracy than your local meteorologist can predict this weekend's weather.

By anticipating what the narcissist's behavior is going to be, how they will respond, and how they will be communicating, acting, arguing, and negotiating, you will be able to prepare yourself. Their patterns will become the foundation for your arguments and leverage. Their need for different forms of supply? Knowledge you can use to your advantage.

You, on the other hand, will not be so easy for the narcissist to predict. Depending upon your relationship, they will assume, incorrectly, that you will continue to operate under that paradigm, whatever it is. There is a very distinct benefit to being underestimated. Keep that in your arsenal and close to the vest. Remember that the element of surprise is critical with narcissists.

Stay on the offensive and focus on you, your mindset, and your side of the fence. Much, much more on that next up in Chapter 8.

What Can You Do Now to Start SLAYing?

1. Which of the strategies here will you start using right away? How?
    - "Just the Facts"
    - "The Middle Finger"
    - "Making a Plan, Stan"
    - "Fluff for Favor, Vomit Later"
    - "COOL Words"
    - What words will you use?
2. What arguments do you anticipate?
    - From the other side (what will they be arguing?)
    - What are your weaknesses?
3. What will you do to be prepared?
4. What will you wear to the negotiation?
5. How will you develop a rapport?

Mantra for Today:

Things are moving in the right direction.

(Or write one of your own that speaks to you....)

CHAPTER 8

Y: YOU ON THE OFFENSIVE, AND YOUR POWERFUL MINDSET

"You've always had the power. You just had to learn it for yourself."
Paraphrased from Glinda the Good Witch in *The Wizard of Oz*

Susan and her husband Steve had a super successful business already when the perfect younger guy, Jackson, came along. Already an employee, but twenty years their junior, he approached them about partnering in the business. He was, at the beginning, in her words, "charming, charming, charming, and perfect in every way." They were so smitten. She said he and his wife were like their kids, and she really thought that eventually this would give her and her husband some freedom so that they could travel and do other things.

Well, within three months of making him a partner, Jackson was becoming a total nightmare. He was making more and more demands. He wanted more money for travel, a housing allowance, and additional benefits. On top of that, he wasn't following through with promises he had made to complete projects, which was causing tension, not only between Jackson and Steve, but also between Susan and Steve. Steve would often defend Jackson to Susan. Eventually, Susan felt that Jackson needed to go, but Steve said Jackson always had some excuse.

Finally, the biggest blow of all came after several months. They found out that he had started another company behind their backs. Not only that, but he had begun poaching several of their employees. A total betrayal. But when they approached him about it, he even lied about that!

They ended up in court and were spending thousands of dollars. She felt utterly defenseless.

Susan said they felt like they could never win. Like she wanted to give up. That is, until she discovered my SLAY Method®. Then it all turned around.

Narcissists make you believe that *you* deserve to lose. Narcissists will tell *you* that you trigger them—and that's *your* fault. That means that when it comes time to battle it out with narcissists, you are conditioned to keep looking over at the other side of the fence (meaning constantly and obsessively looking at what's going on in the other side's camp—in other words, *What's the narcissist up to? What is their strategy? Why aren't they being called out for their behavior? It's not fair that they aren't being ordered to do such and such, and I am! What's going on with their friends?* and so on…). But that, my friends, is a path to losing.

The "Y" in SLAY stands for You, Your position, You on the offensive, Your mindset, and focusing on *Your* side of the argument. This is the most important piece.

You want to be a badass? You want to shift the dynamic? Become fearless against narcissists? You want to win?

You've gotta stop obsessing about their side of the fence. (I know it's hard! Been there!)

While I am going to break this down into two parts, it is still all part of you focusing on you. The two parts are, first, focusing on the strategy and tactics of your negotiation itself, and second, focusing on yourself personally. By "focusing on yourself," I mean your mindset and self-care.

Your Negotiation

In looking at your actual negotiation itself, the biggest shift here is thinking from a place that is offensive. Remember to always keep your eye on your Vision Statements, while implementing your Action Plan, and thinking about how and when you will tactically and strategically introduce your leverage.

For introducing your leverage, timing will always vary, but you will definitely want to keep all your best evidence against them super close to your chest until the very end. You will not want to give anything away until you are absolutely certain that you are ready to divulge what you have.

One of the biggest mistakes I have seen people make over and over—including many lawyers, by the way—is to spend too much time focusing on what's going on the other side.

No football team has ever won Super Bowls by only having a good defense.

You must have a strong offense first; otherwise, no one is actually scoring points. You have to be scoring your own points, not just stopping the other side from scoring theirs.

I once represented a father, Jason, who wanted his four-year-old son, Cole, to relocate back to Florida where Jason was living. Just the year prior, Jason, who had been unrepresented at that time, had lost his custody case when the judge allowed the mother, Chelsea, to move out of Florida to Massachusetts with Cole.

Chelsea then met a new man, who lived in Washington State, and filed a petition to relocate there. That's when Jason hired me. I came in and filed the action to relocate Cole back to Florida. We asked that Jason be named the primary parent, and that Chelsea be awarded visitation over vacations and holidays, as well as whatever weekends during the year she wanted. Basically, we asked for the child's visitation schedule to be for *her*—the one that she was asking the court to order for *him*.

We went to a trial on the issue, and Chelsea's entire case was that Jason was a drunk. She testified that he abused alcohol. She stated with deep vehemence that all of his friends were alcoholics and that "one of them even had a DUI from five years ago." There were photos she had nabbed from Facebook of his family's Thanksgiving, where wine glasses were on the table (none where he was actually drinking from any of the wine glasses, of course). She had hired a private investigator, who showed Jason walking out of a grocery store carrying a six pack of beer. (Ooh, aah!) That was supposed to be her lawyer's major "gotcha" moment.

The problems with her arguments were many. Oh, so many. First, Jason had never had a DUI. Second, she was a former Child Protective Services case worker and yet had allowed Jason to take his timesharing regularly, without question, and unsupervised, so clearly, she wasn't concerned about Cole being in his care. Third, the judge was not interested in what his friends were doing at all. Finally, the *pièce de résistance*? When I asked the private investigator about the date that the six-pack photo was taken? It turned out Jason didn't even have timesharing with Cole that day!

What didn't Chelsea argue that she *should have*? Anything, anything at all, about how fabulous the place she wanted to move to would have been for Cole. She presented no evidence about

Washington State. Nothing about how great the schools would have been for Cole, the neighborhood that Cole would have been living in, the home that Cole would have been living in, the room he would have had, if she or Cole would have had any family around, or if she had any fantastic job opportunities there that would have improved her and Cole's quality of life. She gave the judge absolutely no reason to believe that Washington State would be great, other than that Cole would continue to be with her.

I, on the other hand, painted a picture of what Cole's life in Florida would be like for the judge. Jason testified about how he was still living in the same home that he had bought when Cole was born. Jason's extended family all happily paraded into the courtroom and shared with the judge about how they had weekly family dinners on Sundays. Jason's brother and sister-in-law were also heavily involved with their local Catholic church, including the church's school board. This particular Catholic school went from pre-kindergarten through eighth grade and was known in the town for being one of most sought after by many discriminating parents. That was where Cole would be attending, along with his cousins, should the judge grant Jason primary custody.

Then I argued that the exact visitation schedule that Chelsea was proposing for Jason should be given to Chelsea. If it was good enough for him, then certainly it would be good enough for her. I also had Jason testify that if she ever wanted to move back to Florida, he'd happily give her a fifty-fifty parenting plan. (He gave me some pushback on that behind the scenes, but in the end, he trusted me on that.)

Most of the time, judges have to take some time to rule on custody cases like that. But this time, the judge ruled right from the bench.

The ruling? Immediate return of the child to Florida. Primary custody to father. Done and ordered.

Be offensive. Not defensive. Focus on your case, or your side. This same rule applies, even if it's just a straight negotiation. Remember: certainly bring up the weaknesses of the other side, as I highlighted earlier in this book, but do not have your entire focus be on what the other side is doing wrong.

Stay Focused on Your Facts and Your Vision

Years ago, I worked for a misogynistic, narcissistic, megalomaniacal guy, who, on a daily basis, would say offensive things to me. During the period of time in which I had decided to leave that position but was contemplating my other options, I was doing what comes naturally for humans: I would complain about my job to everyone I knew. Everything about that old job seemed more and more wrong. The guy I worked for couldn't do anything right at that point.

That's when I learned a valuable lesson. My business coach at the time taught me to distinguish the difference between leaving something by making it "wrong" and choosing something new because it was the best option for me. In other words, not "running from," but "choosing to go toward" something that was positive for me. Such a powerful, powerful difference.

Keeping my focus on the positive, not the negative, was the right option for me. I am now reminding you to do the same. You have come this far. Your focus must remain on your strong research and on the summaries you have created by seeing the patterns in the narcissist's behavior, and by remaining focused on your side of the equation, your Leverage, and your Vision Statements.

Now, I know you're reading this and maybe thinking it is so hard when you're continuously getting pummeled on a daily basis by a narcissist. When you are dealing with these types of personalities, it is easy, and I mean so easy, no matter how hard you try not to, to get pulled in, sucked in, and caught up in the day-to-day eruptions, drama, trauma, and chaos they are constantly causing.

In fact, I know there are those days when you've probably been able to measure how the day is going relative to the number of times you've said "WTF" to yourself that day. If it's ten times before you even hit noon, then yeah, it's that kind of a day. I get it. When you're under siege, you just constantly feel on the defensive, and so focusing on their case can be very enticing.

But do not let them have that satisfaction. You are choosing to "go to" not "run from."

Offensive. Not defensive.

Use Their Weaknesses to Your Advantage

Early on in my career, when I was a "baby lawyer," I cut my teeth on one of my first custody cases, where I was representing a devoted dad named Alex. This was during an era where moms automatically got primary custody, and dads got every other weekend and one dinner, on, like, Wednesday night, during the week in divorces.

Well, during the case, the mother, Janelle, actually *left the country* (yes, you read that right: not the state, the *country*) with her boyfriend for a long weekend, leaving her and Alex's three minor children home alone without any adult supervision or care whatsoever. Their twelve-year-old daughter was left "in charge" of their ten-year-old daughter and eight-year-old son.

Now, the twelve-year-old daughter obviously couldn't drive, and even if she could, she didn't have access to a car. This was in the dark ages, so it was way before everyone had cell phones. Janelle had left some food in the house, but she left no money, nor did she alert any other adult that she was leaving the children home alone.

It was not Alex's weekend, so he didn't even know that his kids were all by themselves, fending for themselves, half starving, and trying to figure things out until he got the children back the following weekend, at which point, they slipped and told him. They had been instructed not to tell him, or anyone, of course. He was understandably livid.

It was astonishing that anyone could do such a thing at all, but especially in the middle of a massive custody battle. Wow. The *cojones*! I thought this was a pure gift! *I'm totally using this*, I thought. *This will be the centerpiece of my trial!*

When it came time for trial, we presented all the evidence, including how she had left the children alone. But I also presented lots of evidence about how my client was a stellar dad and how stable he was for the children.

Before my closing argument, I sat with the law partner I worked for at the time. She was one of the nation's top attorneys. I wanted to go over my closing argument with her. After hearing my proposed closing, she cautioned me. I was showcasing Janelle's egregious behavior. My partner said to highlight it, of course, but to argue in my closing that the court should award primary custody to Alex, not as a *sanction or punishment* to Janelle, but because it was in the *best interests of the children.* Again, offensive, not defensive.

Remember that their bad behavior can become part of your leverage, which can be a great thing to use too. It's almost like getting a player from the other side to wear your side's uniform without them even realizing it.

Again, back to scoring points, not just stopping them from scoring.

Use their *weaknesses to your advantage.* That's how it works best for you.

Always take the high road. Always be the one wearing the white hat.

Powerfully Presenting Your Offer

Who should present their offer first? Sometimes, I like to let the narcissist go first—it really doesn't matter, and as I mentioned earlier, it is good to give them options when you can, so that they have a sense of control.

But once it comes time to present your offer, you will want to make sure to ask for a lot more than what you're willing to settle for.

This can be a little tricky with a narcissist. You will want to ask for more than what you're willing to settle for, but not so much that it will inflame them, and they'll just jump up, have one of their little tantrums, and stomp off in a huff. Then you're pretty much done.

And you will want to decide ahead of time what you're willing to give up (remember your "choke point" though). Once you do give that up, you need to do your best Meryl Streep and act like it's the worst thing in the world, like you basically cut off your right arm.

"Oh my! I can't believe they got away with this!" or "Wow, this is so unfair! OMG!"

See what I mean? You will have to check your ego at the door here. If you think you're going to win by letting the narcissist know that you won, then you'll never win. They'll never give in. Because then it would be over; as long as they have decided that you are their target, then they will continue to want to mess with you. What you're really doing is giving them a reason to find a different target.

Also, make sure you never let on what it is that you truly want, because that will be the thing that the narcissist will want to be sure that you never get. You have to play this little game where you throw out a decoy, pretending it's what you really want, and act like the thing you really want is something you don't care that much about.

Again, ethically manipulating the manipulator.

How to Move Narcissists off Their Position and Closer to Yours

1. *Start with areas of agreement and work toward the more contested areas.*

As I mentioned earlier, it will be necessary to establish a rapport with the narcissist. When you want to move narcissists off their position and closer to yours, the way to do that is not to push back against them as hard as you can.

These people thrive on people pushing back against them, so the way to do it is to gently nudge them toward your position.

Think about what happens when you hold your hand up, somebody else holds their hand up, and you push against each other. You can feel that resistance immediately pushing back against your hand. But when you take your hand away, now there is nothing more for the other side to push against. This is what you're doing with narcissists when you are negotiating with them. You want to think about getting them off of their position. One of the ways that you can do that is to start with areas where you think you might probably agree and then work toward the more contested areas.

This way, both sides are feeling like they're getting somewhere. Both sides are having moments of feeling seen and heard. Both sides are feeling as though they are receiving some value, and the momentum will start to build.

Once this happens, when you start tackling the more contested areas, the other side may be more likely to give in on certain things that they might not have been so likely to give in on at the beginning, because they may not want to unravel the entire deal.

2. *Provide reasons why your suggested proposal will get them what they want*

The second way that you can get the other side to move from their position and closer to yours is to provide reasons why your suggested proposal is going to benefit them. This is where your research on both sides of the equation is going to be critical. This is because you're going to be able to demonstrate how much value the narcissist is going to be receiving from the deal.

3. *Demonstrate the risks.*

While you are providing reasons for why your suggested proposal is going to benefit them, you will also be outlining the risks that the other side will face, should they choose to not accept your proposal. Be prepared to outline said risks in painful detail to them. This is where your leverage will come in.

Use Your Leverage

This is where you're going to ethically manipulate the manipulator into realizing that coming to an agreement that day is going to be the best thing for them, meaning that the risks will not outweigh the potential reward that they will be getting.

Here you will unveil what you have accumulated and demonstrate to them why coming to an agreement today will be in their best interests.

Most importantly, you want them to feel that their almighty Diamond Level Supply is threatened in such a way that they will want to protect it. When they do that risk/reward analysis, you want them to think that the continual Coal Level Supply they can get from triggering you, jerking you around, and making your life miserable isn't worth losing their Diamond Level Supply. They will have no choice but to let go of that source of supply, in order to save the Diamond Level Supply.

You want them to conclude that continuing to get narcissistic supply from you is no longer worth the risk of losing the Diamond Level Supply.

Beware of the Mud!

"I'd rather pay you than her." These were the words of a very honest narcissistic client that I once had. In fact, despite my best efforts to bring resolution to his case, he was my client for nearly five years. (In my defense, this was long before I knew anything about narcissism at all.)

Here was a guy who just enjoyed the thrill of jerking his soon-to-be-ex around. He would refuse to provide financial documents from his business, even though he knew he would eventually have to.

He once signed one of her support checks in crayon, with his left hand (he was right-handed).

He would try to goad me into being his patsy in this scheme of making her as miserable as possible. He would say things like "You're going to be so lonely in heaven by yourself, Rebecca."

But here's the rub. *He* was not the only reason that the case lasted as long as it did.

She felt like she needed to retaliate. She would bait him into bad behavior, then file strings of unnecessary motions and pleadings that we would then have to respond to.

They fed off each other.

In the end, between two lawyers, two custody evaluators, two forensic accountants, several mediations, several days of trial, then appeals and cross appeals, they spent hundreds of thousands of dollars. All to end up where they should have started in the first place.

A crazy postscript to that story…they ended up reconciling!

Here's another story for you.

My husband, a business litigation attorney, represented a golf course country club that was sued by a man who said he was injured while playing golf. Now, he didn't slip and fall on the course, mind you. No, he got into a fist fight with another golfer while he was there playing golf, and somehow, in his mind, that translated into the injury being the fault of the club. A total narcissist.

The lawyer for the man who got into the fight was also a narcissist. (I always say that clients and lawyers are like dogs and owners. They always seem to find ones that look like them.) This man's lawyer took the case on a contingency basis, meaning that he would not be paid unless there was some sort of settlement.

Even though it had done nothing wrong, the club offered twenty thousand dollars in the beginning, just to try to settle the case quickly. The lawyer said no. The club upped their offer a bit to something like thirty thousand dollars. The lawyer again said no. The club gave their final offer: fifty thousand dollars to this guy who got into a fight on a golf course and probably had too much to drink that day. Fifty thousand dollars for basically causing his own misery. They said no.

So, the fight club dude and his lawyer ended up litigating the hilt out of this case. Remember: the lawyer wasn't getting paid unless there was a settlement of some sort. The club was owned by the largest developer in Florida, so they had very deep pockets. There were depositions in New York City, travel expenses, and more. It went on for months. They even did a three-day trial.

And guess what.

They lost completely. No settlement at all. In fact, it was even worse. The fight club dude? He had to pay the club's legal fees as well as the legal fees for the other dude he got into the fight with. Then what did the fight club dude do? Filed for bankruptcy. No one got paid a dime. Except my husband and the other lawyers for the club.

Yep. Fight club dude really should have taken the fifty grand.

The moral of the story? Don't get into the mud.

Don't get sucked into "being right" or having conversations with yourself that involve the phrase "it's the principle of the thing."

Those two phrases don't generally lead to a peaceful, efficient resolution. Know what does though?

Using your Strategies and Leverage. Keeping your eyes on your Vision Statements.

Focusing on You

We really have saved the best for last.

It's time to focus on *you.* I have said this over and over again throughout this book, but this is the most important place for me to say this again: 99 percent of winning the negotiation between the narcissist and you happens before you enter the room.

But guess what? There's something even more powerful.

Every bit of winning at the game of life happens right inside of you. You see, the battle with the narcissist is just that: the battle. Eleanor Roosevelt said, "No one can make you feel inferior without your consent." Once you understand that, then you really start to make the shift.

I want to make a *distinction* here for you.

Here's what's *negotiable*:

You can negotiate contracts. You can negotiate issues or terms. You can negotiate any *topic* you want.

Here are your *non-negotiables*:

You will never negotiate your self-worth. You will never negotiate your self-respect. You will never negotiate *who you are.*

Remember how Glinda the Good Witch said to Dorothy at the end of *The Wizard of Oz* that she always had the power to go home, but that she just had to learn it for herself? I remember thinking, as a kid, *What a rip! How stupid is that?* But now, of course, I totally get it. The brilliance of the entire story.

At the end of every single one of my YouTube videos, I say, "Today is a great day to start negotiating your best life." That's also the name of my podcast: "Negotiate Your Best Life." At the beginning of my podcast, I say sometimes the very first negotiation we do is with ourselves for our own self-worth. How many of you can relate?

The real secret to beating narcissists, communicating successfully with narcissists, and negotiating our best lives does not lie outside ourselves. It's what I call an "inside-out" job. By that, I mean you really must start by feeling your own power inside, then work your way out.

What happens is that we do our own "confirmation bias" all day long. As children, we start telling ourselves we aren't worthy, then we go through life, through our day-to-day interactions with people, looking for evidence in reality that this is true, and then confirm that our beliefs are facts. "See, I knew I was different," "Yup, I do suck at losing weight," "I definitely am a piece of crap," "I always mess up relationships," or whatever it is that you say to yourself subconsciously or even consciously.

We have something in our brains called the Reticular Activating System. It only allows a certain amount of information to get through at a time, sort of like a filter. You know how, when you buy a car, like, say, a brand-new red Toyota Corolla? Suddenly, all you see are red Toyota Corollas all over the road. That's because you programmed your brain to notice them. That's what you do when noticing your worth too. The more you start winning, the more you start to notice your wins.

The great news is that your brain is just like the CPU of your computer. It can totally be reprogrammed. You can absolutely reprogram it so that you are the powerful expression of what's possible for yourself.

If you're an empath, which more than likely you are, then this is one of the hardest things to do. Steps 1, 2, and 3 were all about stopping the conditioning, then pivoting, and then starting to feel powerful enough to communicate in an authoritative way with toxic people. Regardless of whether the relationship is business or personal, there is actually a symbiotic nexus between a narcissist and empath. As an empathic person myself, especially one who landed in a business relationship with a narcissist, I found this quite interesting.

Why Narcissists Target Empaths

An empath is a person who feels deeply for others, who has tremendous care and compassion, and as a result, has many people around him or her. Empaths generally are smart, creative, attractive, and charismatic. This is why narcissists want to be around them. They want to attach themselves to a person who is perceived by others as valuable, and they also want someone who will take care of them.

Narcissists also want someone who will put them on a pedestal and allow them to appear to be in control, and who will make all their needs and wants the priority over anything else. Empaths will generally allow this to happen, because they will "go along to get along." Many times, empaths have their own core wounds, which have given them codependent tendencies, and this codependence makes it easier for them to trauma-bond with narcissists.

This all results in a deeply destructive cycle, where empaths are pouring love, attention, support, and value into the narcissists. The narcissist seems like they need fixing, because they will say they were a victim of a horrible childhood. But it ends up being a well that has no bottom, because the narcissist never ends up reciprocating. They sprinkle some love bombing in here and there. But they're really like leeches or parasites who will suck the empath dry, and when there's nothing left to suck out, then they head to their next source of supply.

When you are an empath with your own wounds and your own inherent, deep-seated feelings of low self-esteem or low self-worth, then you somehow subconsciously think that you weren't worth loving or being in a business relationship with, or that you caused this behavior somehow. Maybe it will cause you to not trust yourself again in your work or in your personal life.

Narcissists can leave you with deep psychological damage. You can see how both personality types feed some sort of needs in the other person, none of it healthy, and none of it sustainable. It's like eating junk food every day. You might stay alive, but you'll feel like total crap.

In negotiations or any kind of interactions with narcissists, you need to know that this pattern will continue unless you interrupt it. You are going to feel pulled back in, like a magnet. Remember: the narcissist knows your weak spots, they know what to do to suck you back into their lair of insanity, and they will use those weaknesses to the fullest.

If you're an empath, then this is one of the hardest things to do. Why?

Reprogramming Your Brain

Your brain is like the CPU of your body. When we were children, we were exposed to certain stimuli, and then we drew conclusions. For example, let's say that a child wanted to sit on her grandmother's lap. Her sibling was already on their grandmother's lap, but she dove in anyway. At that moment, her grandmother exclaimed, "I can't have both of you on my lap at the same time! Off!" The child might have drawn the conclusion that she wasn't lovable. Now, the adult version of her could probably look at that scenario, think how ridiculous that was, and see how that had nothing to do with being lovable. It obviously was because this older woman didn't want two rambunctious kids on her lap at the same time!

But this is what we do as humans.

In that moment of being pushed off Grandma's lap, that little girl might have concluded, *I must not be lovable.* Then, maybe that same little girl went to school a couple of days later, and the teacher didn't pick her for something she wanted to be chosen for. Confirmed: not lovable. Then two weeks later, kids picked teammates for a game of kickball, and she was chosen last. Yup. Not lovable.

Then it would become the refrain of the song that never ends. Remember Lamb Chop, the puppet who sang the song "The Song That Doesn't End"? That's what your faulty thoughts are. It's even worse than "The Song That Doesn't End" though.

That little girl would then grow up to be a woman and have those feelings of unworthiness buried deep within her. She would think they were facts though. Esther Hicks, the spiritual teacher who speaks through her spirit guides she calls Abraham, says, "A belief is just a thought that you keep thinking," and that's what keeps you from having the life that you want. It's all in your mind.

Dr. Joe Dispenza, in his book *Breaking the Habit of Being Yourself*, explained that inside our brains are patterns of neurons that fire together. Our brains want to be efficient, so especially during childhood, neuronal patterns are formed, because the brain says to itself, "Oh, we're thinking that way again. Ah okay. Got it!" If we are presented with the same stimulus over and over again, our brain learns to respond the same way. It's like a pattern of dominos. The first one hits, the rest fall in line, and then these patterns become hardwired into the brain. The brain has been programmed.

This means that you have this shame, this secret, this underground knowledge that no one else has, that says you are unworthy in some way. Then you spend the rest of your life either trying to prove you are worthy or trying to cover up the fact that you're unlovable or whatever you think it is that your issues are, by being super successful or figuring out other ways to mask your dirty little secrets. Brené Brown calls it "hustling for your worthiness."

But of course, here's the rub: you never were unworthy in the first place. All your conclusions were based upon flawed reasoning to begin with.

What happens in relationships with narcissists is that those old neuronal patterns get triggered. When they start devaluing you, making you feel small, lining up those flying monkeys, and manipulating you, you go right back to being your ten-year-old self, or whatever age you were when your initial unhealed trauma took place.

As soon as they accuse you of being a lousy father, mother, wife, husband, business partner, or whatever, those dominos fire, triggering the patterns, your limbic brain is engaged, and *kapow*: your feelings of unworthiness come flooding back. You subconsciously or consciously start to think, *Oh no, the world is going to see the truth: that I'm unworthy.*

On the other side of the fence, narcissists, while they have no actual empathy, are masters at reading what your weaknesses are and then using those against you. They sniff it out like sharks sense blood in the water. They search for ways to strike out against you, especially once you become Public Enemy Number One.

This means that when negotiating or communicating with the narcissist, you're going to have shut them out, while at the same time rewiring your brain so that new neuronal patterns take over, so that your old neuronal patterns are no longer running the show.

You can do this. Remember. Just decide. Kill off any other possibilities.

A Note about the Narcissist's Brain

Before we move on to how to become the most powerful person in the room, I wanted to mention to you that the above is exactly what is going on in the narcissist's brain too. This is why they are prone to bouts of narcissistic rage and tantrums. Remember all the way back in Chapter 2, when I explained how a narcissist's brain was formed? I explained that when their narcissistic injury gets triggered, their narcissistic rage comes flying out. *This is exactly why*.

They are being triggered. The domino has been set off.

When a narcissist's limbic brain is triggered, they lash out and become destructive. Sometimes they are destructive even to themselves. They do not see you or feel anything about you. They twist everything to fit their narrative and will never see reason, ever, so don't bother trying to demonstrate it to them, especially when they're in this state of rage.

What types of things trigger narcissists? To begin with, just like you, anything that consciously or subconsciously reminds them of their past traumas. They also absolutely hate being rejected. Narcissists also all have a major fear of abandonment and looking stupid or weak. The one to remember the most, as I mentioned earlier in the Leverage section, is that their Diamond Level Supply sources are their biggies, and potentially exposing them is the biggest trigger of all.

Victim Versus Victor: People Will Think What You Tell Them to Think

No one likes to walk around and say that they are a victim. I certainly don't. As I mentioned, I have been the target of two covert narcissists—both of whom were very stealthy in their execution. While I was still in an active relationship with them, I saw them as the problem, not me as the victim.

However, each day, as things would happen in my business or in our family situation, I would get very upset. I would then stew about it, be up late at night ruminating about it, and spend countless hours talking about it with my husband, my friends, or my family. But if someone had said to me during that time that I was being a victim, I would have pushed right back and been defensive about it.

I certainly thought of myself as a strong person. I had been a litigator for nearly twenty years at the time. I had gone up against some of the most formidable opponents and won. I had been named one of the top litigators in the country. To me, being accused of being in "victim mode" was tantamount to being accused of being weak and being controlled, and maybe it even would have exposed my shame, my feelings of self-doubt, and my low self-worth.

But the undeniable truth was that these people were getting to me. I wanted to avoid talking to them. I was avoiding confronting them. I told myself it was because I was keeping the peace, or maybe I was making too much of something. Covert narcissists are very insidious and stealthy, and they are masters at engaging in the kinds of underhanded behaviors that give them plausible deniability. This means that when you tell other people about what they are doing, it either doesn't sound that bad, or it doesn't sound like that person because everyone else's experience of that person is so radically different. It's like death by a thousand cuts. They are excellent at gaslighting and making you think you're the one who is crazy. Maybe that's why I didn't speak up.

The cold, hard truth is that when you say, "They are making me feel bad," or "They are ruining my life," you are making yourself out to be a victim. Sometimes, that's hard to hear.

When you decide you are a victor, you also get to decide what people think of you.

Here is the way I learned that lesson. I had been practicing law, then went and spent a couple of years at Morgan Stanley as a financial advisor. I thought it would be a better lifestyle for me, as a young mom. (It didn't really turn out that way.) A couple of years into that gig, a friend of mine who was a family law attorney approached me about taking over her practice. She was leaving town and was dropping it in my lap if I wanted it.

That was when I decided to go back to practicing law, to start my own practice. At that time, I hired a business coach. She taught me one of the most important lessons in my life, which I carry with me to this day, and I really want you to carry it with you.

Always.

I almost didn't start the practice, because I really was concerned that the small, very affluent, sometimes very judgy community of Naples, Florida, where everyone knows everyone else, was going to think I was a total *flake*. Why?

Well, because I had been a lawyer for a few years, then went off to be a financial advisor, then I went back to being a lawyer. I thought everyone was going to think, *This chick! She doesn't know what the hell she wants!*

My business coach just looked at me, and with conviction, she said, "People will think what you tell them to think." Then she went on to say with even more conviction, "You can tell them to think that you're a flake, *or* you can tell them to think that you're the only family law attorney who has a financial background, and therefore you're obviously more qualified than any other family law attorney in this community."

She paused for effect.

"Which story would you like to tell?"

So, guess which story I told?

Within two years, I had one of the top family law practices in the state, representing people of wealth and influence. People who clearly would not have hired a flake.

Thus, I will submit to you that in every moment when you are thinking about what the narcissist is doing, or talking about what the narcissist has done or not done lately, you are not allowing yourself to be the best self you can.

Focus your energy back on yourself instead. People will think what you tell them to think.

Tell the narcissist and everyone else in the world that there's a new game in town.

You have to override that "victim brain." Sometimes, though we might not want to admit it, we can get addicted to being a victim, because there can be a payoff for being in victim mode too. Here are some of the benefits:

> *You get attention.*
> *You get to be right.*
> *You get to point the finger at the other person and make them wrong.*
> *You don't have to take responsibility for your actions.*
> *You get others to feel sorry for you and see you as the victim*
> *You get others to think the other person is the bad one, and you're the good one.*

The other part of this is that somehow, in our minds, we think that if we let go of pointing the finger, then they end up "getting away" with whatever it is that they did—that, somehow, our holding on to being right or being the victim of their abuse holds them accountable.

Well, guess what? It doesn't.

Here's the flip side of being in victim mode: if you are in victim mode, then you are not in control of your life. You are saying to the world, to the universe, and to yourself, that you aren't the one making decisions; that someone else is.

If you want to be the decider of your life, then you need to make a choice right here and right now that you are no longer going to be in victim mode.

Ideally, you always show up as the elite, powerful version of yourself.

Mental Pivoting

One of the things that has worked well for me is pivoting, like we talked about in Chapter 4. We want to retrain our brains to think about something else as soon as the negative thoughts flow in. Remember: if there's no other alternative, then they will go right back to the thoughts they know.

Self-Care

There's a lot that goes around about "self-care," and half the time I think either none of us really know what that means, or we don't know how to do it if we do. When I think of self-care, I often think of people lying in a spa, wrapped in towels, with cucumbers over their eyes. Sounds fab, but who has time for that on a regular basis?

For those of us who are busy all the time, dealing with our lives—families, careers, or both—even finding a few minutes of quiet time can be a stretch. I know, because I've been there. But when you're in a relationship with a narcissist, it's way worse.

Self-care when dealing with a narcissist is something totally different. It's not just about caring for yourself, it's also about protecting yourself, starting to heal, and preserving your strength and your sanity, so that you can be at optimum condition when dealing with one of the toughest fights of your life. We talked about several methods in Chapter 4, and here are a few more.

Don't Take Anything Personally

Think of the narcissist as the raging bull in the china shop. There is a lot of destruction, but it's not like the bull meant to go for one particular Lladró or piece of Wedgwood. It just happened to be in the way. The narcissist fixates on people, but they just happen to be the people who landed in their space. The truth is that they will suck supply from whomever they can find.

Remember that even when they attack you personally, it's really not a personal attack; they just hate themselves deep down inside. They hate anyone who dares to come near them too. *The way people treat other people is always a direct reflection of how they feel about themselves.*

Good or bad. It never has to do with you.

This is one of the hardest things for empaths *not* to do sometimes. We take everything personally.

Self-Soothing Therapies

There are some self-soothing therapies that you can do that are based in somatic therapy. Somatic therapy was developed to help trauma survivors release tension stored in the body on a cellular level to help with the healing process. There have been several practitioners in this area, but Dr. Peter Levine is probably the most well-known expert. There are so many different types of somatic therapies that you can choose from, but here are a few easy ones to start with:

- **Hands Over Heart and Belly**: When you first wake up in the morning, place one hand over your heart and one hand over your belly. Notice the weight of your hands and notice your breathing. Then say to yourself, "At this moment, I'm okay and I am loved." Breath in and out. Do this at least three times.
- **Hug Yourself**: Cross your right arm over your chest and over your shoulder, making sure to cover your heart. Then cross your left arm over your right shoulder. Hold tightly for as long you wish, but for at least one minute, to feel contained and safe.
- **Meditate**: If you don't meditate, I highly recommend that you try it out. Even if you start with one minute a day, then work up to two, and then to five minutes a day, it will make a huge difference in your life. Your mind is going a million miles a minute all the time. Giving it a few minutes to just rest will help you find that place to center when you're in times of stress, craziness, and anxiety throughout the day.

If you're like most people and have a hard time learning how to focus and stop your thoughts from flying in, then there are a lot of apps out there that can help you get started. There are even plenty of YouTube videos on getting started with meditation now that are totally free. Just start. Get up a few minutes earlier and give yourself the gift of starting to meditate a few minutes a day. It has literally changed my life.

- **Deep Cleansing Breaths**: When we are stressed, we don't even notice that we start to breathe in a much shallower way, which actually causes us to take in much less oxygen. This means that our cells build up more carbon dioxide and over time this can lead us to feeling more sluggish, or even worse, can lead to medical conditions such as kidney or lung issues.

All you need to do is to just stop every so often during the day and take in a deep breath, as deep as you can go, and then let it out, as far as you can go. Then repeat the process a few more times. I like to visualize while I am doing this. I visualize that I am taking in positive energy while I am inhaling, and then, while I am exhaling, that I am getting rid of all the toxicity and negative energy that is stored inside of me.

The great thing about this exercise is that no matter how busy you are, you can do this. You don't need money, special clothes, or anything to get started. Start right away. Do it several times a day. You can even set your phone timer to go off a few times a day to remind yourself to do it.

Gratitude Practice

One of the reasons I love doing my podcast, aside from getting to help people on a global scale, is that I get to meet the most incredible people. I have interviewed dozens of people now. One of the most thrilling people for me to meet and interview was the great Bob Proctor. I am so grateful I got to meet him before he transitioned to his non-physical state. What a thrill. If you haven't had a chance to catch that interview, definitely go check it out. It's on both my YouTube channel and on my podcast, anywhere you listen to podcasts.

Many things he said to me that day have stuck with me. One of them was the importance of a daily gratitude practice. To this day, I begin the day by writing down ten things for which I am grateful. It has made such a tremendous difference in my life.

There is scientific research on the impact of a daily gratitude practice on the brain. Studies have shown that a regular gratitude practice can help to improve your mental well-being, impact your level of optimism, and even lower rates of stress, anxiety, and depression. Other studies have even found a connection between expressing gratitude on a regular basis and an increase in self-esteem and a more positive body image over time. Clearly there is a direct connection between gratitude and life satisfaction overall.

When we are in the state of gratitude, we are in the state of receiving. We are open. We are realizing that there is abundance in our lives. By realizing that, we place ourselves in a position to receive more.

Conclusion

Narcissists sense weakness and fear, zero in on it, then go right in for it.

On the other hand, the more confident you are, the higher your vibration, the less they will want to be in your space, because they will be more and more intimidated.

There will be less and less supply source from you.

Remember: they are more afraid of you than you are of them.

By focusing on *you* and your mental health, you will undoubtedly be stronger and more confident in your negotiations and your communications.

Eventually, you won't even care what the narcissist thinks, because you will just be the strong, confident, powerful version of yourself.

Like an oak tree. Firm. Strong. Grounded.

But, just in case you're still panicking a teeny, tiny bit, next up in Chapter 9, I'm going to give you some super simple, grab-and-go tools for SLAYing your negotiations with the narcissist, to make sure that dragon knows it is so f*cked.

What Can You Do Now to Start SLAYing?

1. Your Negotiation (use another piece of paper or a journal):
    - What are the strengths of your case/negotiation? (Remember to think of having a strong offense, as well as a good defense.)
    - What are the weaknesses of your case/negotiation?
    - What are the strengths of the other side's position?
    - What are the other side's weaknesses?

- What will your first offer be?
- What will your choke point be?

2. What exercises will you start using to help you focus on being a victor instead of victim?
    - Mental Pivoting
    - Self-Soothing Therapies
    - Hands Over Heart and Belly
    - Hug Yourself
    - Meditate
    - Deep Cleansing Breaths
    - Gratitude Practice

Mantra for Today:

I deserve care and am worthy of it.

(Or write one of your own that speaks to you….)

CHAPTER 9

THAT DRAGON IS SO F*CKED

"Courage is not something that you already have that makes you brave when the tough times start. Courage is what you earn when you've been through the tough times and you discover they aren't so tough after all."

MALCOLM GLADWELL FROM *DAVID AND GOLIATH*

"How to Make a Narcissist Panic." That's the name of my top performing video on YouTube. Does that tell you something?

How many times have you fantasized about beating that narcissist? Or making that narcissist panic? There are so many times when I was lying awake at night that I thought to myself how nice it would be if the Earth just opened up and the narcissists just happened to disappear.

If you've read this far, you have felt like you were David and the narcissist was Goliath. For those unfamiliar with the Biblical story of David and Goliath, that's the one where David was a young, inexperienced boy and Goliath was a huge giant. Goliath was a bully who wanted to fight David, showed up with all sorts of weapons, and fully expected to win. But surprise! David took Goliath down! He slayed him! How did he do it?

He believed that he could.

David was able to SLAY Goliath. He had Goliath panicking! With the right tools and the belief that you can defeat your narcissist, you can SLAY too. If you go in believing you'll win, Goliath is already damned.

Put another way, now that I've gotten you to the point where you've formulated your strong (S)trategy, you've created invincible (L)everage, you know how to (A)nticipate the narcissist's actions and reactions, and you know to focus on (Y)ou and your position, you have the basics for communicating and negotiating with your narcissist. You have the tools now, you know how they think now, and your moves are more calculated than their own. By the time you step into the arena with the narcissist, you've carefully planned the negotiation. You are ready to SLAY. That means that, while the narcissist may not know it yet, they should be panicking.

But maybe, just maybe, some small part of *you* is still panicking—just a wee bit.

That's why, in this chapter, I wanted to give you some quick ideas at a glance. Here, you can just grab a few more super simple tools for SLAYing your negotiations with the narcissist, just to be sure you know you have everything you need to win.

Depose to Expose

Remember that the narcissist will protect and defend their Diamond Level Supply at any cost. One trick that I have discovered is that if you have a litigation case that is active and open, let the narcissist know in some subtle way that you will be speaking with their top shelf, Grade-A Supply—people that they may not want you to speak with—through a formal process called a deposition.

A deposition is a process where a witness is compelled to answer questions under oath. The questions would be asked by an attorney with a court reporter present.

Using the power of a subpoena, an attorney can compel anyone to show up at the meeting to answer the questions. Now, can the witness object? Yes, absolutely they can. But that person would probably have to hire a separate attorney to file some sort of Motion for Protective Order on their behalf and then set that motion for a hearing in front of the judge. If your narcissist doesn't want this person involved, it will be a major source of irritation for them, and thus a huge potential source of leverage for you.

Additionally, during the questioning process, the scope of questions that can be asked is pretty broad. The attorney can ask anything that can lead to the discovery of admissible evidence. They can't ask about anything that is totally irrelevant to the case or about privileged information. For example, they can't ask about a person's sex life if that has nothing to do with anything in the case, or what a person's lawyer advised about an issue, but otherwise, the door is wide open.

This scares the bejesus out of narcissists of course. They do not want you sniffing out their best sources of supply. No sirree, Bob. They want you far away from their good supply sources, especially if they've been telling them all sorts of lies about how awful you were and creating some sort of new narrative.

Finally, during the depositions, if your lawyer is really good, he or she can kind of stealthily feed information to the narcissist's Diamond Level Supply that the narcissist might not want them to know, by asking the questions in the right way. There is a way that this must be done. Here is an example.

I had a coaching client named David, who had a small travel agency that he had built on his own. He met Peter at a travel conference, and they hit it off immediately. It seemed to be a perfect match. Peter also had a small travel agency with several agents. When they went back home, they remained in touch and became fast friends. Peter was very charming and told David of how he had just had to go through a transition because his former business partner had relocated, and so he was really in a bind dealing with all the operations on his own. David was struggling with managing the operations and also the training and sales, so Peter immediately suggested that they become partners. He said that training and sales was his strong suit and that he'd handle all of that and that David could handle operations.

Within a month of meeting at the conference, David found himself agreeing to merge his business with Peter's business, even though they were in different areas of the country. While he had his reservations, each time he tried to express them, Peter would assure him that he had nothing to worry about, and that it would all be great. Yes, there were red flags. There were times during the process when Peter was supposed to do certain things to effectuate the merger and he didn't do them, but he always seemed to have a good reason: his wife was sick, or one of his employees was out of the office, so he had to cover for him, he said. So, David ended up handling what Peter was supposed to do, even at the beginning of the merging process.

Then, as they got deeper into the process, David started to notice other things. He asked Peter to sign a partnership agreement. Peter said that he would but then would never get back to David on the terms. When David pressed him on it, Peter would become angry and say that he hadn't had an opportunity to speak with his lawyer and accused David of not trusting him. He even made David feel guilty for asking, by stating that this was no way to start a partnership. Big red flag! But David didn't want to rock the boat. He'd already announced the merger to his employees and to his clients. *Too late to turn back now*, he thought.

The following month, David wanted to go ahead and schedule the sales trainings for the new agents they were hiring. He asked Peter the specifics of how the trainings would be scheduled and how Peter planned to facilitate them. For example, did he plan to have them in person? Did he want to do them at one location and have the agents travel to that location? Would they last for a full day? Would he do them monthly? Peter said that he had all of that under control, and that David did not need to concern himself with that.

David then proceeded with handling the operations end but quickly realized after a few months that they were hiring new people who weren't getting trained, so he began scheduling trainings. Peter would then show up at the trainings, step in, and take control, leading all the employees to believe that he had organized them, never giving David any of the credit. David even ended up finding and recruiting new salespeople, which had been something Peter was supposed to do. This led to a huge boost in revenue for the company. Peter then took credit for that too.

David finally had enough. He was starting to think he might want to go a different direction. When Peter felt David pulling back, David realized Peter was plotting against him by lining up some of the key employees against him. He realized that Peter was actually even planning to start another company of his own.

When David came to me, he was scared. He didn't know where to begin to negotiate with Peter. We formulated a plan. We needed to create some leverage. In this case, the leverage would be that Peter would not want to be exposed to the employees as the one who didn't actually contribute anything to the company.

That's when we decided that David should approach Peter with an offer to buy him out of the company for a fair price, or alternatively, he would sue him to dissolve the partnership, which would mean that all the employees would then have to be deposed and questioned about what they knew about the company. During those depositions, the attorneys would have the opportunities to ask questions such as "Were you aware that Peter did not contribute to the growth of the company?"

That's how you use the "depose to expose" method. It can definitely be very effective with narcissists.

David went to the negotiations with two documents in his hands. In one of his hands, he held a buyout agreement. This was Peter's Option A. In the other, he held a Petition to Dissolve a Partnership, which was to be filed in the courts the next day if Peter didn't sign the buyout. The petition was drafted by an attorney already and ready to go. This was Peter's Option B. Peter knew David was absolutely ready and totally prepared for either option. He was unblinking.

Peter decided to settle. He chose Option A.

Feed Their Ego, Free Your Soul

Another way you can come to a resolution is to fashion the conversation in such a way that you allow them to come to the conclusion you want, so that they think that it is *their* idea. Ask them their opinions on things. Tell them they are so much better at thinking things through than you are. They want to be able to take credit for the idea.

You're going to be asking for way more than you want in the first place anyway, so if the final deal is the one that they offer, then that's fine. Let it be. They will have to be the one who is the designer of the deal.

Remember to play the long game here. Sometimes you have to let the narcissist have the last word on the surface, if you end up getting what you wanted anyway (ethically manipulating the manipulator). Feed their ego. Free your soul.

It's Wise to Use the Element of Surprise (Especially in Litigation)

Priscilla was a divorced executive assistant in her forties. Her children were grown, and she had a peaceful life with her cats and her girlfriends. Weekends meant yoga, grocery shopping, Weight Watchers, maybe a dinner with her parents, and catching up on laundry. When Howard, a wealthy retired CEO in his sixties, came along, she was less than inspired at first. But he was quite persistent, and then he swept her off her feet.

He took full control of her life immediately. He insisted she quit her job and give up her own place to move in with him within a month. He said he would "take care" of her. He wanted them to be free to travel together. They traveled all over the world. While in front of the Taj Mahal, he went down on one knee and proposed. She couldn't believe she had found her Prince Charming. They had only known each other for three months.

When they got back to the states, she was surprised to learn that he had already spoken to his lawyers and had a prenuptial agreement already drawn up. "Just a formality," he said. They'd be together forever, of course, and he would always "make sure she was taken care of."

Within a month of the wedding, her life became a living hell. He became verbally and mentally abusive. Then, a few years into the marriage, she found out that he had hidden bank accounts in Switzerland. She only discovered this because the IRS found out, and he had to tell her. Apparently, they had been filing joint tax returns to save taxes, but he hadn't been declaring the income from the Swiss bank accounts, and now was possibly on the hook for back taxes, penalties, and worse, even criminal prosecution.

He hired the best possible lawyer to defend himself of course—and then dropped the hammer on Priscilla. He told her that she was on her own. No lawyer for her. Ahem. *Excuse me?* Yes, exactly.

Her next stop? My office. She filed for divorce. We served him as he was walking out of his Park Avenue apartment in New York City. He was shocked!

At mediation, Howard wanted Priscilla to take exactly what the prenuptial agreement terms gave to her. Well, the problem with that was that the prenuptial agreement required full financial disclosure—which he clearly had not given her, since the Swiss bank accounts were not listed there.

Priscilla had massive leverage.

The attorneys' fees to litigate the validity and enforceability of the prenuptial agreement would be high. Howard would lose that fight. The prenuptial agreement would definitely be set aside.

Howard chose to settle. Priscilla got paid—a lot more than what the prenup terms called for.

When you're dealing with a narcissist, you absolutely must use the element of surprise. If you don't, then the narcissist will plot and plan against you.

This is especially true if you are litigating against a narcissist. Bearing that in mind, I want to give you a few things to remember when using the element of surprise if you are preparing to go to court against a narcissist. Think of these as your "tools-at-a-glance" to live by if that's your world right now.

1. **Hear No Evil, See No Evil, Speak No Evil: Nothing Ahead of Time**. Act like you have nothing on them and feign total ignorance at all times. If you have a lawyer, then you can always say that you are letting the attorneys handle everything and you just want what's fair under the law, and put it all on the attorneys.

2. **Appear Naive**. If they try to hoover you and want to get back together, act like you might be interested. The weaker you can appear, the more you can encourage them to misbehave. I know you think this will allow them to "get away" with doing things that they shouldn't, but you must again think of the long game. You want opportunities to document patterns, and you don't want to tip your hand. If they know what you want, they will go after that.

3. **Pretend You Want Something Else**. The narcissist will want to make sure you don't get what you want and will therefore go after something if they think it's what you want. Therefore, pretend you want something else, then feign disappointment when you don't get the thing that you didn't really even want in the first place. Feed them information that you want to feed them. It's all about ethically manipulating the manipulator.

4. **Always Wear the White Hat, Even When You Don't Want To**. There will be many times when it will feel like the narcissist is "getting away" with things. Remember there are no little "fairies" that jump out in your living room or office and go to the narcissist, "Aha! You didn't behave!" The only person with any power over anyone else is a judge if there is a case open. So just keep documenting like crazy and know that karma will take

its course eventually in the courtroom. But if you don't conduct yourself nicely, then you will both just look like two kids who aren't behaving to a parent. You need to be the one who is totally unscathed and clean. Keep smiling. Wish them well. Stay above the fray. Be humble, kind, and gracious. You are the Dalai Lama or Mother Teresa. The more you do this too, the worse the narcissist's behavior will get, so it will only work in your favor.

5. **Respond, Don't React**. Remember to never let your emotions take over. That's what they want. With a narcissist, they are always throwing that bait out there to collect evidence against you. Plus, they seriously just get off on seeing you squirm. Don't give them the satisfaction. Also, everything you write, text, or email is a potential trial exhibit.

6. **For Presenting Offers, Use Option A Versus Option B**. When presenting offers to narcissists, never send settlement proposal letters back and forth. That is a total waste of time. Always wait until you have your best leverage ready to go, then get them into a position where they are totally squeezed and boxed in; physically is best, such as a mediation setting. Then present two offers. One is Option A where they sign that day, which is the option that you want, and then Option B is the one that they do *not* want, which is where their Diamond Level Supply will be exposed. They have to know you are dead serious and ready to go. Do not get to this point until you are absolutely and totally ready, or your entire strategy will have failed.

7. **Do Not Give Away Your Best Evidence Until You Have To.** There will be deadlines for exchanging

information and exhibits for your case and for court. At those points, you will have to give the other side information. Even then, I only disclose what is absolutely necessary. Always, always, always remember that the more you can use the element of surprise, the better. Don't give anything away, especially your leverage, until you absolutely must.

The most important theme here is not to be lulled into thinking that the narcissist is a regular, reasonable person. Yes, you can give the narcissist who hurt you compassion, but send them light from a distance. From far away. You need to take care of yourself.

Keep your laser focus on your Vision Statements and continue to employ your Strategy and your Action Plan, use your Leverage, and stay on the offensive. In short, focus on SLAYing. Remember to move through Steps 1, 2, and 3. This is how you will win. That's how you get the narcissist to want to give you what you want, without backlash.

That's when you'll start to notice something else too. *You* will have changed. You will have transformed.

That's how you become a SLAYer for life. That's up next in Chapter 10.

What Can You Do Now to Start SLAYing?

1. Depose to Expose. If you are litigating a case, think about your narcissist's Diamond Level Supply sources. Are there people that could potentially be "Deposed to Expose"?
2. Feed Their Ego, Free Your Soul. Are there some areas that you could ask the narcissist's opinions about, in order to

help bring about resolution in your negotiation? If so, what are they?

3. It's Wise to Use the Element of Surprise. If you're in active litigation against the narcissist, how will you be implementing the following?
    - Be like the monkeys: see, hear, and speak nothing ahead of time.
    - Appear naive.
    - Pretend you want something else.
    - Always wear the white hat, even when you don't want to.
    - Respond, don't react.
    - For presenting offers, use Option A versus Option B.
    - Do not give away your best evidence until you have to.

Mantra for Today:

I have a plan, and I know it's working.

(Or write one of your own that speaks to you….)

CHAPTER 10
SLAYER FOR LIFE

"Set your life on fire. Seek those who fan your flames."
RUMI

Congratulations! You did it! You SLAYed. Even if all you did so far was just read this book, give yourself a pat on the back.

Acknowledge yourself. Allow yourself time to be grateful for the gift of information, education, empowerment, and enlightenment that you gave yourself. It is not an easy journey to start to shift the dynamic of power, especially if you've been in a long-term relationship with a narcissist, so kudos to you for taking this journey. This may be the most important one you've ever taken.

Also, let's take the time to thank each other for being in each other's lives. While I may have never met you, I want to thank you for allowing me to be a teacher to you and allowing me to be the vessel of information for you. I honor you and our relationship.

Remember to always look for opportunities for which to be grateful, and to express your gratitude every single day. You are no longer a victim, nor are you a target. Be grateful for that. It is impossible to express gratitude and be unhappy at the same time. By expressing gratitude, you instantly pivot, and you instantly raise your vibrational energy.

You can find moments of gratitude in whatever situation you are in. This is what will literally change your vibration in any moment. Any time you catch yourself feeling like a victim, find something to be grateful for. There is always, always, always something to be grateful for. Even if it's just clean air, a warm bed, or clean water. Just stop and give yourself just a few moments a day.

At some point in your healing journey, you may even come to a place where you are able to feel gratitude for the narcissist. Now, I know what you might be thinking, but hear me out. I'm certainly not telling you to go have tea with the person and start hanging out again. What I'm saying is to understand that, from a spiritual perspective, we were meant to have trials.

So regardless of whether you had an actual *trial* with the narcissist or whether your "trial" with the narcissist was a trial of life, it is in these moments of adversity that we are defined. The narcissist is really just a representation of what you can overcome. Strength doesn't come from what you can do, it comes from overcoming the things you couldn't.

We need the rainy days to appreciate the sunny days. Our souls wouldn't be able to grow if we didn't have opportunities to learn.

Of my most favorite nature metaphors is the lotus flower. In the Chinese culture, it is one of the most revered flowers, and considered to be one of the most beautiful. Interestingly, though, it will only grow in mud. Once it starts to bloom, the petals only open one by one. How beautiful is that? All of us as humans bloom, even from mud, and learn our lessons, throughout our lives, one by one.

The stronger you become, the better you become, because then you realize: that thing you thought you could never do? You did it! Everything you want in your life is right outside of your comfort zone. Oh, and by the way, that comfort zone? That's a lie too. Your brain is telling you to stay in your comfort zone to keep you small.

Stop playing small. Did you know that 95 percent of the thoughts you are having today are the same exact thoughts you had yesterday and the same thoughts you're going to have tomorrow? If you've ever seen the movie *Groundhog Day*, it's just like that, but we don't even realize it.

You Were Born for More

The real reason that your soul couldn't breathe under the regime of the narcissist was because it knew it was born to create. *You* were born to create.

There can be no doubt whatsoever that once you get on the other side of SLAYing the war with the narcissist, your soul will be ready for the next level of growth in your journey. You can overcome anything.

Take time each day to get still. Listen to your truth. Listen to your soul. Get to know your soul. As Gary Zukav teaches in his book *The Seat of the Soul*, once you set your intention and learn how to align your personality with your soul's intention, that's when you will truly feel whole and complete, because you'll feel authentic power, which is true power that can never be taken away from you—that power that is from your soul.

It's time to create your next opportunities, to serve your soul at its highest level.

This is what you are meant to do. I believe it is your duty to use the gifts you have been given to serve the world. You now have the opportunity to rise above. You can take your pain and trauma and help others to transform theirs. You are being called to be empowered and inspired.

Today Is a Great Day to Start Negotiating Your Best Life

For those of you who follow me on a regular basis, you hear me say this in every single video and in every single podcast: wherever you are in your journey, this is your moment. This is your jumping-off point. It is never too late.

It's time to figure out what comes next for you. It's time for you to start majoring in the majors of life, instead of the minors of life. This means it's time for you to focus hard on the things that mean the most to you. They are what some people call the core "Fs" of life. Here they are in no particular order:

Family
Faith
Finances
Friends
Fun
Fitness

I like to add one that sounds like an "F" sound but starts with a "Ph": Philanthropy. What I want you to do now is to grab a pencil and paper and, referring to the above list, write down what you believe is the highest and best version of yourself and your life in each of the areas above. Be super specific. I have done this, and it is very powerful for manifestation. Really take the time to think about each area by asking yourself questions like this:

For family, you might think about:

What is your relationship like with each of your family members?

What does a typical day look like for you?

For faith, you might think about:

What kind of relationship do you have with God/spirits/the Universe/love (or whatever name you have for a Higher Power)?
What kind of meditation practice do you have?

For finances, you might think about:

How are your finances?
How much money do you save regularly? How do you invest it?
What kind of clothes are you wearing?
Where are you living?

For fun, you might think about:

What do you do for fun?
How do you feel about yourself?

For friends, you might think about:

Who are your best friends?
How do others feel when they are around you?

For fitness, you might think about:

What kinds of things are you doing for self-care?
What kind of fitness routine do you have?
What does your body look like? How much do you weigh?

For philanthropy, you might think about:

How much do you donate to charity?

These are just some questions to get you started, and this is not meant to be an all-encompassing list. Please feel free to add in anything else you want.

Once you complete that, then start creating a plan for how you will attain that elite version of yourself in each one of those areas. For example, you could break your plan down by where you will be in one year, then break it down further by months and by days. In this section, you can apply what we learned about how to create Vision Statements in Chapter 5. Make sure that each category is covered.

This is how you will begin to negotiate your best life.

This is how you will start to feel whole and complete again. Remember at the beginning of the book how we talked about how you want to feel?

Once you conquer that narcissist, you can conquer anything.

Here is what some people who have successfully applied the SLAY Method® and gotten to the other side have said:

> "I finally had the strength to run and never look back! The other day, I almost forgot his name!"
>
> Debbie

> "I feel amazing; I do. I feel amazing and I haven't felt that way in many years. I know I'm here for a reason, and it's for the greater good, and I will be of help to others. It's changed my life."

Necole

"I never thought I would be in the place that I am now. Focusing on the Y, the *You*, is the most important part. It's not going to be easy, but it is going to be worth it on the other side. The SLAY framework works. You have so much chaos in your life. To have something really simple—that was the basis of a new life for me. There is no easy way out. But that was it. But it is so worth it to get out and take your power back. You can do it!"

Chikodi

"I feel lightness and joy every day."

Ryan

"Viktor Frankl says, '…suffering ceases to be suffering at the moment it finds a meaning.' I was being demonized on a daily basis. Through the SLAY program, I suddenly realized those patterns of behavior, and everything made sense. That was such a relief. Then it was a relatively painless process. Legal separation signed. My way of giving meaning to what I've gone through now is by helping others."

Christian

"I successfully negotiated against the narcissist in my divorce. But then the most surprising and amazing thing happened after the negotiation

> was over. My fear disappeared. Not just of the narcissist. But in my life. I now feel more confident and empowered in every aspect of my entire life. It is truly a miracle."
>
> Marilyn

I have thousands more from men and women around the world, but I just wanted you to have a sampling of how you will feel too. But you won't get there unless you take the steps to get there. There is a famous Chinese proverb that says, "The journey of a thousand miles begins with a single step."

Yes, it can be daunting. But yes, you can do it.

Jack Kornfield said in his book, *Buddha's Little Instruction Book*, "The trouble is, you think you have time." Someday means never. Someday is a "habit" of thinking that you'll never get to. Get into a habit of creating action steps, then executing the steps. Even if you just take a few small steps at a time, you will feel a whole lot better about yourself.

Your word to yourself means more than anything. Have integrity and keep the promises that you make to yourself. As soon as you do that, you will see that everything in your life will change.

Integrity should be your love language. Without integrity, nothing works. Integrity is the foundation, the core of every relationship. Even a building needs a foundation that is strong. If there are cracks in it, people say that the integrity of the foundation is compromised. The same should go for your words to yourself. If you make a promise to yourself to make your bed every morning, then make your bed every single morning, even if you are at a hotel, and even if the cleaning lady is coming that day. Just to keep your word to yourself. It's about the energy, the karma, and you keeping your promises to yourself. Because if you can do it on the small things, then you will with the bigger things too.

You will start to feel that you are worth it, that you are valuable. Then others will start treating you with that same level of value. The world will start showing up for you in a different way. Experiment with it for a day, then two days, then three. Give it a year. See how your life changes.

Remember you and you alone create your value.

You have the power.

You've always had it.

Every time you decide you're a winner, you are a winner.

That's when you truly SLAY.

The Y, The Deciding Factor, is *you*.

What Can You Do Now to Start SLAYing?

1. Focus on majoring in the majors of life, instead of the minors of life.
    - Family
    - Faith
    - Finances
    - Friends
    - Fun
    - Fitness
    - "Ph"ilanthropy

Take the above list and write out the most elite version of yourself and your life in each of the areas above.

2. Once you complete that, then start creating Vision Statements in the format we learned about in Chapter 5. For each one, describe how you will achieve the outcomes you want in one of those major areas. For example, you could break it down by where you want to be in one year, then break it down by months and then by days. Make sure that each category is covered.
3. Write down how you feel now that you have SLAYed. How has your life shifted? How have you changed as a person?

Mantra for Today:

I know my future is bright. I'm worthy of it, and I'm ready to SLAY. (Or write one of your own that speaks to you....)

"SO, WHAT DO I DO NOW?"

Congratulations! You've read the book! Or maybe you listened to it. But now what? Are you wondering what to do next or where to go from here?

I promised that I would guide you every step of the way, and I meant it. The hardest part is trying to do it all by yourself. When you're feeling like you're lying on the side of the highway, trying to crawl out the ditch, as if you are a carcass that the narcissist vulture has picked clean of the narcissistic supply, the prospect of attempting to go up against that same person over and over again in negotiations can be overwhelming.

Reading this book has been an excellent start. You now have an awareness of how a narcissist thinks and how they condition their targets. Additionally, you have the SLAY framework and tools in your hands and at the ready. You also understand that, in order to shift the dynamic of power, there are three steps: first, there is Step 1: "Don't Run," which is where you stop the conditioning. Second, in Step 2: "Make a U-Turn." Finally, in Step 3: "Break Free," you will start powerfully walking forward in the other direction.

In order to really be able to see meaningful changes in your life though, that critical step of "execution" is what's going to make the difference for you. In order to do that, because of what you've likely experienced in dealing with narcissists, you will need support.

While I have been guiding you throughout this book, I want to continue to give you that critical support. That's why I have given you a lot of links to free resources as we have gone along, including a link for a free Masterclass. Join me via this link right here: www.icanslay.com. It's totally free and offers you additional incredible support. You can sign up right now. I do it several days a week at different times to accommodate any schedules. It's live, and I even do my free live Q and A at the end.

Remember that there are other free bonuses and resources at www.slaythebully.com/resources. One additional bonus I want to give you is a SLAY-at-a-Glance Chart, which is also at that same website. Make sure you check out this page and grab all your free gifts. They come with your purchase of this book.

I also have a free private Facebook group at https://www.facebook.com/groups/narcissistnegotiators/ which I highly recommend that you join for additional support and access to an amazing and supportive community.

Please also feel free to subscribe to my YouTube channel—www.youtube.com/rebeccazungesq—and follow me on Instagram @rebeccazung and TikTok @rebeccazung.

It's my mission to help as many people on this planet as possible break free from toxic relationships and negotiate their best lives.

Finally, one thing I know for certain is that you and I were meant to cross paths. Wayne Dyer said there were no coincidences. It's all meant to be. It's been my honor to be in your life for this very important journey.

I send you light and love as you sprout from this mud and become a fully blooming lotus on your own.

I hope to meet you one day and hear your story of triumph.

With deepest gratitude,
Rebecca Zung
Chief SLAYer

SLAY THE BULLY: HOW TO NEGOTIATE WITH A NARCISSIST AND WIN

Key Ideas at a Glance

- **S** stands for **Strategy**. This is where you create your Super Strong Strategy—your foundation and your GPS for your entire negotiation. You begin with the end in mind. Here you will create your Vision and your Action Steps.
- **L** stands for **Leverage**. This is where you will motivate, squeeze, and incentivize the narcissist into wanting to come to a peaceful resolution with you, by understanding what makes them tick. Narcissists don't think like non-narcissistic people, and they are not motivated by the same things as non-narcissistic people, so you *cannot negotiate with them like you do non-narcissistic people*. Period. If you create an invisible fence around the narcissist and do this the right way, by creating a smart Strategy and

then building the right Leverage, you can have the narcissist begging you to resolve your negotiation.

- **A** stands for **Anticipate**. This is where you get two steps ahead of the narcissist in anticipating their behavior, their arguments, and what is motivating them.
- **Y** stands for **You** and **Your position**. There are really two elements to this part of the framework. The first part is the tactical portion, where you must understand that you must think offensively. The second part of this is focusing on *you* and shifting your mindset, so that you 100 percent believe that you can win.
- Narcissists' brains do not function in the same way that non-narcissistic people's brains function, because of the complex trauma to their limbic systems as children. Thus, we absolutely must have a different paradigm in dealing with them. This is so critical to understand when communicating and negotiating with narcissists.
- People who are *targeted* by narcissists are also often at a disadvantage because they have been traumatized by narcissists. This is because narcissists use many tools and tactics to destabilize and take control of their targets.
- We need to *educate* not just laypersons who are interacting with narcissists (and their targets), but also attorneys, judges, anyone who works in the court system, managers at all organizational levels, C-level executives, medical professionals, teachers, clergy, and even many mental health professionals. There is a crucial difference between people who are not narcissistic, who are much more likely to endeavor to reach an actual resolution during the negotiation process, and people who suffer from narcissistic traits or tendencies, who may actively endeavor to torpedo the process, because they are trying

to take the other person down (often even *at their own expense*). These people do *not* want a resolution, because that would mean an end to their *supply source.*

- Experts estimate that potentially up to 15 percent of the world's population either has narcissistic personality disorder, possesses narcissistic traits or tendencies, or has other types of antisocial personality disorders which may cause them to lack empathy. To put that into perspective, there are approximately 7.9 billion people on the planet currently and about 333 million in the United States. If each one of the 15 percent of the global population emotionally abuses just three people in their lifetimes, that results in approximately 3.4 billion people in the world, or 150 million in the United States, being the victims of a toxic personality. That is why it feels like it happens to nearly all of us.
- When it comes to communicating or negotiating with narcissists, we have been going about it *all wrong.* This is precisely why the regular way of negotiating *fails.* Narcissists are driven by one thing and one thing only: narcissistic supply. This is the Key to the Kingdom. Narcissistic supply is anything that feeds a narcissist's ego.
- There is hierarchy to narcissistic supply. There is what I refer to as Diamond Level Narcissistic Supply: how they look to the world. Diamond Level Supply is Grade-A Supply. Narcissists will protect and defend this form of supply at any cost. This is anything having to do with the outside world, such as reputation, prestigious careers, impressive friends, accomplishments, and huge bank accounts.

- The second form of supply is what I refer to as Coal Level Narcissistic Supply. This is the dark underbelly of supply. This is insulting behavior, purposely demeaning others, or triggering people. Also important, but if push comes to shove, they will give this form up to save the Diamond Level Supply.
- There is a huge myth when it comes to negotiating with narcissists! People think toxic narcissists just want to win. That myth is dead wrong. They do want to win, but they also enjoy the process of watching you squirm and intimidating you. That myth only considers one form of supply: Diamond Level Supply. It totally forgets about and discounts Coal Level Supply.

They do want to win, but they also want to manipulate you, trigger you, make you squirm, and just generally make your life miserable. You can't negotiate in a normal way with someone who wants to make your life miserable. The normal rules of negotiation will not work and will never work with narcissists, because they want *both* forms of supply.

Narcissists sure as hell hate to give up any of their supply—*willingly*.

The key to leverage will be figuring out what source of Diamond Level Supply is more important to them than the Coal Level Supply that they get from making their target's life miserable. You create a situation in your negotiations that will make the narcissist *feel* like their Diamond Level source of supply *might* be exposed. You threaten a supply source that is more important to them than the satisfaction they get from jerking you around.

Tactically, you hold back on actually exposing them, because if you do, then your leverage is gone. This formula always works.

You are ethically manipulating the manipulator.

- **Three steps to Shifting the Dynamic of Power.**
    - **Step 1: Don't Run.** This is where you stop the conditioning from the narcissist, by stopping yourself from retreating, and stop walking backwards.
    - **Step 2: Make a U-Turn.** This is where you pivot, and you turn around. This is where you will create a plan for negotiating that will start to shift the dynamic of power and create your leverage.
    - **Step 3: Break Free.** You will start walking forward. This is where you will actually present your offers and start speaking. It is throughout this period that you reclaim your sense of self and your power, slowly but surely, knowing that somewhere inside, your power never left.

- You can discover what kind of narcissist you're dealing with, then actually predict how they will behave and how to be two steps ahead of them.
- Always stay on the offensive and focus on your side of the fence.
- **Here's what's** *negotiable*:
    - You can negotiate contracts. You can negotiate issues and terms. You can negotiate any *topic* you want.

- **Here are your** *non-negotiables*:

    - You will never negotiate your self-worth. You will never negotiate your self-respect. You will never negotiate *who you are.*

- You must 100 percent believe you can win. You and you alone create your value.
- People will think what you tell them to think.
- Regardless of whether you have an actual *trial* with the narcissist or whether your "trial" with the narcissist is a trial of life, it is in these moments of adversity that we are defined. The narcissist is simply a representation of what you can overcome.
- Your soul knows you were born for more. Once you conquer the narcissist, you can conquer anything.
- It's time to create your next opportunities and to serve your soul at its highest level.
- Today is a great day to start negotiating your best life.

ACKNOWLEDGMENTS

To God and the Universe be the glory. I am simply the vessel through which You communicate. Thank You.

To my husband, John. Thank you for a quarter of a century of love and life. What a journey this has been since you picked me up in Analysis of Evidence class at the University of Miami School of Law so long ago.

To my children (and now grandchildren), Alexander, Nicholas, Danielle, Emma, Trey, Catalina, Joseph, Max, and Summer. You are my reason. My everything. My reason for everything I do. Always have been. Always will be.

Thank you to Freddy and Sara for being incredibly supportive partners to my babies and parents to our grandbabies. Love you so much.

To my parents, Max and Madeline. Thank you for giving me an incredible kickstart in life. I am eternally grateful.

To my brother, Michael. My first best friend. Love sharing a gene pool with you.

To all of my extended Zung family—so grateful to have grown up surrounded by your love and support, which continues every day to this day. I know how blessed I am. So much love for you.

Thank you, Caroline and Debi. The best, best friends on the planet. My soul sisters forevah!

Thank you, Ed Cederquist for sharing your invaluable business wisdom and for your guidance, support, and friendship.

Thank you, Kelly Townsend. Eternal gratitude.

Thank you, Jack Long, for having been the absolute best law partner and mentor anyone could ever ask for.

To Chris Moujaes, my Libra and 888 partner in crime by day. How did I ever survive without you dear friend? Eternal gratitude for keeping me sane.

There are many, many others in my life who give me daily support and love on a regular basis. Too many to name here. You know who you are. I am deeply, deeply grateful for each of you.

To Lynsi Snyder-Ellingson, Owner of In-N-Out Burger, for partnering with me to bring Slay Legal Aid to life and for Susan Sly and Bret Lockett for being our founding board members on this philanthropic mission that will change lives.

Thank you to my literary agents at Dupree Miller, for seeing the light in this project then helping me bring it to the world.

To Debra Englander—I believe there are no coincidences. We were meant to reconnect on this project and bring it to life. Thank you.

Thank you to the narcissists and bullies in my life—you've been great lessons.

To each of the millions of people who allow me to serve them each day via YouTube, Instagram, one of my programs, or any other medium, thank you. I am grateful to be in your life and honored to be able to support you.

ABOUT THE AUTHOR

Author Photo by Stephanie Vu

Rebecca Zung has been honored by US News as a Best Lawyer in America and is a globally recognized expert in negotiating with narcissists with nearly 40 million views on YouTube in just three years. Also an expert in negotiation, her book *Negotiate Like You M.A.T.T.E.R.: The Sure Fire Method to Step Up and Win* remains on the Amazon bestseller list. She has been featured in numerous widely known media outlets, including television, print and podcast interviews and her opinions remain highly sought after. Her resources have and continue to transform the lives of many around the world.

But her journey wasn't always easy. Married at nineteen, she had three children by the age of twenty-three and divorced, before going to law school as a single mom while still in her twenties. She went from being a single mom and college dropout to becoming one of the most powerful lawyers in the country. Now, she is committed to helping people everywhere, negotiate their best lives.